The Complete Home
Decorating
Idea Book

The Complete Home
Decorating
Idea Book

Thousands of Ideas for Windows, Walls, Ceilings & Floors

By Kathleen S. Stoehr

CHARLES RANDALL INC.

Published in the United States by: Charles Randall, Inc., Orange, California
Distributed in Great Britain by: Gazelle Books
White Cross Mills, Hightown, Lancaster, LA1 4XS
United Kingdom
www.gazellebookservices.co.uk/

The publisher has made every effort to ensure that all suggestions given in this book are accurate and safe, but cannot accept liability for any resulting injury, damage or loss to either person or property whether direct or consequential and however arising. With regard to the source guide you may wish to confirm colors, patterns, sizes, names or contact information. Variations in color may occur during the printing process. The publisher will be grateful for any information that will assist in keeping future editions up to date.

Printed in the United States of America

ISBN 1-890379-16-6

Editor: Kathleen M. Stoehr
Book Interior, including photo research: Chemistry Creative
Cover Design: Diego Linares
Cover Credits: Cover, Seabrook Wallcoverings (*Top image*); (*Bottom left & Middle*) Armstrong World Flooring; (*Bottom right*) Jamie Gibbs & Associates/Michael Goldberg, Classic Decor. Back Cover, (*Left column*) Armstrong World Flooring; (*Middle column*) Brunschwig & Fils; (*Right column*) Hunter Douglas, Armstrong World Flooring; Author photo courtesy of Hanna K. Stoehr. *Please refer to the Index for additional information.*

Library of Congress Cataloging-in-Publication Data

Stoehr, Kathleen, 1960-
  The Complete home decorating idea book : thousands of ideas for windows, walls,
ceilings & floors / by Kathleen S. Stoehr. -- 1st ed.
      p. cm.
   Includes index.
   ISBN 1-890379-16-6 (pbk.)
   1. Interior decoration. I. Title.

NK2115.S699 2007
747'.3--dc22

2007033509

Contents

Introduction

WE BEGIN OUR REDECORATION PROJECTS WITH SUCH HOPE, AND THEN...ABOUT HALFWAY through the wallpaper stripping, the spackling and sanding of blemishes on the walls, the indecision we reach as we decide between Fabric A and Fabric B ... a lot of projects sputter. I know it's true because I've been there. I've looked at my walls in disgust because I can't seem to get past the removal of the very pesky wallpaper paste lines ... for months on end. I've put up temporary shades, using big metal office clips to hold them up, because I can't seem to decide between a shade or a blind. It happens to everyone.

Window treatments ... turn to page 08

But my goal in assembling this extensive, exhaustive book on all things related to decorating your surfaces is to save you the trouble I have experienced throughout the years. Instead of having to walk through countless interior design shops looking for inspiration, I have assembled the most important aspects of any room into one book. Want to decide what color you wish to paint your walls before

this is your full service design store

you walk into a paint store? Turn to page 172. How about window treatments? Well, that would begin on page 08. Floors? Got that, too — see page 308. What I have tried to do is take away the distractions of shopping, the wandering, the second- guessing. This book is your interior design store and I have compiled over 1250 photos to put at your disposal to mix, match and develop the style and feel of interior that suits you best.

Divided into four major sections, *The Complete Home Decorating Idea Book* begins with my personal favorite, window treatments, and then moves into wall decoration (and there's plenty more than paint, as you probably well know), then flooring and finally — the surface most everyone forgets until it's too late — the ceiling.

So page through. Enjoy. Dream a little bit, even. Just don't let your room wait too long.

Kathleen S. Shoehr

Ceilings ... turn to page 278

Wall coverings ...
turn to page 152

Floor coverings ...
turn to page 308

Window Treatments

THE RIGHT WINDOW TREATMENT WILL DO AWAY with all of the negatives. It will allow privacy when needed and reveal the outdoors when you wish to embrace the day. Through motorization, easy manipulation is as simple as pressing a button. Need a focal point? No problem. Window treatments range from understated to elegant, modern to absolutely sumptuous, wildly creative to downhome friendly. We hope these following pages will inspire your creativity!

Traversing draperies coupled with woven wood Roman shade on adjacent wall make a bold statement. Photo courtesy of Sarah Barnard Designs

Shutters

Shutters

Shutters

Shutters: bi-pass door

Shutters: bi-fold door

Shutters: French door

Shutters: unusual shapes

Shutters: unusual shapes

Shutters: unusual shapes

Blinds: horizontal

Blinds: horizontal

Blinds: horizontal

Blinds: horizontal

Blinds: vertical

Blinds: vertical

Blinds: fabric vane horizontal

Blinds: fabric vane horizontal

Blinds: fabric vane vertical

Curtains & draperies: arch top

Curtains & draperies: arch top

Curtains & draperies: banded

Curtains & draperies: banded

Curtains & draperies: bishop sleeve

Curtains & draperies: café curtain

Curtains & draperies: café curtain

Curtains & draperies: café curtain

Curtains & draperies: cuffed

Curtains & draperies: cuffed

Curtains & draperies: cuffed

Curtains & draperies: fan pleats

Curtains & draperies: fan pleats

Curtains & draperies: fan pleats

Curtains & draperies: flat panel

Curtains & draperies: flat panel

Curtains & draperies: flat panel

Curtains & draperies: flip topper

Curtains & draperies: flip topper

Curtains & draperies: flip topper

Curtains & draperies: flip topper

Curtains & draperies: goblet pleat

Curtains & draperies: goblet pleat

Curtains & draperies: goblet pleat

Curtains & draperies: grommeted

Curtains & draperies: grommeted

Curtains & draperies: grommeted

Curtains & draperies: pinch pleat

Curtains & draperies: pinch pleat

Curtains & draperies: pinch pleat

Curtains & draperies: pinch pleat

Curtains & draperies: ring top

Curtains & draperies: ring top

Curtains & draperies: ring top

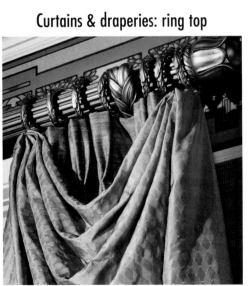

Curtains & draperies: ring top

Curtains & draperies: rod pocket

Curtains & draperies: rod pocket

Curtains & draperies: rod pocket

Curtains & draperies: rod pocket

Curtains & draperies: ruffled rod pocket

Curtains & draperies: ruffled rod pocket

Curtains & draperies: ruffled rod pocket

Curtains & draperies: ruffled rod pocket

Curtains & draperies: styling tape

Curtains & draperies: styling tape

Curtains & draperies: tab top

Curtains & draperies: tab top

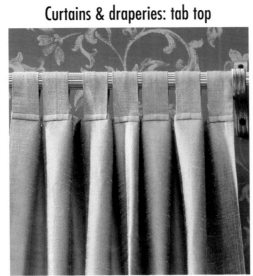

Curtains & draperies: tab top

Curtains & draperies: tent fold

Curtains & draperies: tie top

Curtains & draperies: tie top

Curtains & draperies: waterfall

Curtains & draperies: waterfall

Curtains & draperies: w/attached valance

Shades: accordion/pleated

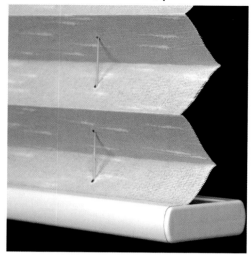

Shades: accordion/pleated

Shades: accordion/pleated

Shades: austrian

Shades: austrian

Shades: austrian

Shades: balloon/cloud

Shades: balloon/cloud

Shades: balloon/cloud

Shades: bottom up/top down

Shades: bottom up/top down

Shades: cellular/honeycomb

Shades: cellular/honeycomb

Shades: cellular/honeycomb

Shades: matchstick

Shades: matchstick

Shades: matchstick

Shades: roman/roller

Shades: roller

Shades: roman/flat fold

Shades: roman/flat fold

Shades: roman/flat fold

Shades: roman/flat fold

Shades: roman/london

Shades: roman/relaxed

Shades: roman/relaxed

Shades: roman/relaxed

Shades: roman/soft fold

Shades: roman/soft fold

Shades: roman/soft fold

Shades: solar

Shades: solar

Shades: woven wood

Shades: woven wood

Shades: woven wood

Top treatment: awning

Top treatment: awning

Top treatment: cornice/mock

Top treatment: cornice/soft

Top treatment: cornice/soft

Top treatment: cornice/upholstered

Top treatment: cornice/upholstered

Top treatment: cornice/upholstered

Top treatment: cornice/wood

Top treatment: cornice/wood

Top treatment: scarf/pole mounted

Top treatment: scarf/pole mounted

Top treatment: scarf/pole mounted

Top treatment: swag/board mounted

Top treatment: swag/board mounted

Top treatment: swag/pole mounted

Top treatment: valance/balloon; cloud

Top treatment: valance/balloon; cloud

Top treatment: valance/butterfly

Top treatment: valance/butterfly

Top treatment: valance/pick up

Top treatment: valance/pick up

Top treatment: valance/pick up

Top treatment: valance/pleated

Top treatment: valance/pleated

Top treatment: valance/pleated

Top treatment: valance/pleated; shaped

Top treatment: valance/pleated; shaped

Top treatment: valance/rod pocket

Top treatment: valance/tab top

Top treatment: valance/tab top

Top treatment: valance/tie top

Top treatment: valance/tie top

Top treatment: valance/triangle

Decorative: bead trim

Decorative: bead trim

Decorative: bead trim

Decorative: bracket

Decorative: bracket

Decorative: bracket

Decorative: braid/welt cord

Decorative: braid/welt cord

Decorative: braid/welt cord

Decorative: border/tape

Decorative: border/tape

Decorative: border/tape

Decorative: finial/glass

Decorative: finial/glass

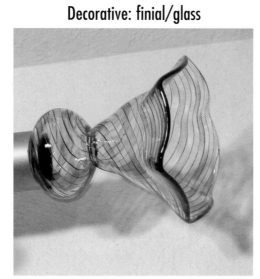

Decorative: finial/metal

Decorative: finial/metal

Decorative: finial/metal

Decorative: finial/metal

Decorative: finial/wood

Decorative: finial/wood

Decorative: finial/wood

Decorative: fringe/brush

Decorative: fringe/bullion

Decorative: fringe/bullion

Decorative: fringe/bullion

Decorative: fringe/ribbon

Decorative: fringe/ribbon

Decorative: grommet

Decorative: grommet

Decorative: grommet

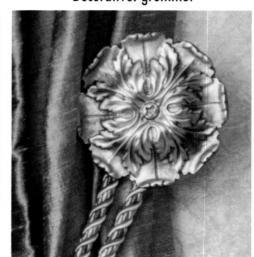

Decorative: holdback

Decorative: holdback

Decorative: ring & rod

Decorative: ring & rod

Decorative: shade pull

Decorative: tassel

Decorative: tassel

Decorative: tassel

Decorative: tassel

Shutters

FOR THE HOMEOWNER WHO VALUES PERMANENCE, shutters are the penultimate choice, a combination of beauty, precision light control, warm, traditional appearance — and a life expectancy unmatched by most other window coverings.

Combine shutters with fabrics to soften their hard lines or leave them beautifully, distinctively elegant; choose from a variety of styles and configurations, from plantation, roller, accordion, arch top and more. Plus, many shutter styles offer insets such as glass, woven grass and reeds.

Natural and warm, well-insulating and capable of being stained or painted to match just about any decor, shutters are a wise choice for any interior.

Shutters can be completely casual — or as shown in accompanying photographs, entirely elegant.

Compact in small areas — a great choice.

Shutters complement the room's decor.

Fan top with shutter.

A description of shutter components is in the text below.

The value of shutters lies in their extreme durability and classic beauty.

About shutters

There are many types of shutters but whatever kind you choose, note that the same four components are usually present. As I explain each component, take a look at the image directly above this paragraph. I have placed a number next to each so you have a visual reference.

1. Rails. These pieces are structural and range in height from approximately two inches to about 4.5" depending upon the height of the panel and the size of the louver.

2. Louvers. Rotating on a pin and connected together by a tilt bar, these individual pieces can vary in size from a typical standard 1.25" to over four inches. depending upon the material used and the type of shutter product.

3. Tilt bar. Connected to each of the individual louvers in the center, the tilt bar controls the light, privacy and ventillation associated with the shutter. Usually moves only up and down.

4. Stiles. The right and left structural pieces, which aid in holding the shutter together. Usually about two inches wide and holds the pins in place that connect to the louver.

You may not be surprised when I mention that shutters are available in faux wood as well as solid wood. You might think that sounds odd, but consider where you might want to use a shutter product — for example, where high humidity or moisture may be an issue. How about a bathroom or kitchen area? A laundry room or basement? Exactly. Faux wood and vinyl shutters are moisture and fire resistant, they will not warp and can also cost much less than their wood counterpart.

There are some drawbacks, of course. If you are looking for a product that looks just like wood, you

A perfect treatment for a simple area.

Single swing out shutter.

may be disappointed in some of the lower end products; you may also experience some color fading over time — especially if you have ordered white shutters and they are exposed to direct sunlight; and finally, the range of color is somewhat limited, being the product cannot be painted.

Wood shutters come with their fair share of problems as well — humidity and moisture resistancy problems at the top of the list. Plus. should you decide to paint the shutter, you may find you have a problem with "sticky" louvers. Finally, there is always the potential for cracking, warping and bowing. Remember, this is a natural product that will expand and contract depending upon the environment, so don't think for a moment that your wood will not be affected.

On the plus side, you can't beat wood for its natural, warm beauty, high structural integrity and of course, the fact that it's recyclable. Wood can be painted or stained to match any decor and, of course, when maintained properly, wood will last a lifetime.

To finish this section, I'd like to point out that there are other materials beyond wood, faux wood and vinyl. There is metal, which is typically used when the shutter is used on the exterior of a home — and generally in those areas that suffer from high wind and rain. There is a product called Polycore, in which an aluminum core is inserted into the center of a solid polymer as it is being extruded. This reinforcement allows shutters to be constructed in lengths up to 36" wide, maximizing light control. Be sure to do your homework and check out these other materials: Polywood™, a synthetic wood substitute and Thermalite™, a solid, non-toxic synthetic material made of a dense polymer foam.

Finally, there are so many different types of shut-

Shutters can open with the louvers only, or swing wide for an unencumbered view.

A modern approach for the kitchen.

ters available. Consider this short list when you are looking for your next interior shutter treatment.

- Cafe. A smaller-style shutter used to cover only the bottom half of a window, for a combination of privacy and sunshine.
- Eyebrow. A shutter that is wider than it is high and resembles the shape of an eyebrow. You will see a shutter like this used on larger windows that have a great deal of architectural emphasis.
- Panel. This is a shutter that operates on a track system. I suppose you could liken it to something you might see on a closet, only this shutter would slide in front of a glass door in order to afford privacy to the home's occupants. It may also have an attractive insert, such as fabric, woven wood or glass.

- Plantation. With a name evoking the mansions of the southern U.S., plantation shutters have louvers over two-inches wide. Even four inches wide is appropriate. This allows for the breeze to circulate throughout the room well when the shutters are wide open, and when closed, offer a great deal of light control and privacy.
- Shutter "blinds" truly do resemble wood blinds, conbining the larger louvers of a shutter with the ease of blind operation.
- Sunburst shutters are typically constructed in the shape of an arch with louvers radiating like rays of the sun from a central point, usually on the bottom edge of the piece.

Bright white shutters with two-inch louvers.

A few more things

Today, shutters can be found both indoors and out, offering more than just protection from the elements: exceptional beauty, terrific insulation, a variety of light control options and a life expectancy unmatched by most other window coverings. Plus, you can consider shutters an investment — most are appraised into the value of a home.

Combine shutters with fabric to soften their hard lines or leave them beautifully, distinctively elegant. Comb through the variety of options: plantation, roller, accordion, arch top, Bermuda and more. With louvers from as little as one-quarter of an inch to as wide as five and a half, there's definitely a shutter to fit your needs.

Shutters installed over just 75% of the window is an intriguing way to address privacy but always allow sunlight.

Fitting perfectly into a bay window; softened with draperies.　　Sun passing through the louvers creates interesting patterns.

Just an upward tilt of the bar will open louvers wide.

Great for compact areas.   Combined with fabric, hard shutter edges are softened.

An old world feel, with shutters that can swing open and bring the outdoors in.

When open, shutters allow the architectural beauty to shine.

A great choice for the dining area.

Light control with louvers, swags to soften.

An excellent combination of beauty and practicality.

Design by Diana Apgar, Interiors by Decorating Den

Imagination abounds with light lime shutters.

Casual elegance for a large glass expanse.

Design by Carol Allain, Interiors by Decorating Den

Design by Diana Apgar, Interiors by Decorating Den

Perfect for a compact area.

Vinyl shutters are a great choice for high moisture areas.

(above) Enhancing the rich, chocolate tones with wood. (below) A masculine look.

(above) Woven wood panel inserts instead of traditional louvers. (below) A strong, eye-catching statement.

Sleek bay window shutters are perfect for the kitchen.

White shutters bring energy and appeal.

Streamlined bank of shutters is as modern as it gets.

Water resistant shutters for the bathroom area.   Clean and permanent — great for an office environment.

Specialty shutters showcase the latest technology.

(above) A perfect choice for small, accent windows.

Bright white and ideal for a bathroom.

Great for compact areas.

Wide louvers create dramatic appeal.

Shutters on a door makes for a great solution
when concerned about privacy.

Design by Jane Speroff, Interiors by Decorating Den

(above) Small areas require compact treatments. (below) Sleek and subdued plantation shutters.

(above) Sleek look combines well with casual decor.

Bright white shutters pop against green walls

A lovely combination of shutters and ring top draperies.

Great choice on a large window wall.

Classic specialty shaped shutters in a sunny area.

(below) Large louvers offer maximum sun and viewing when open; full privacy when closed.

Curtains & Draperies

THERE IS NOTHING MORE INVITING AT A WINDOW than a set of curtains or draperies. This could be considered a relatively strong statement but truly — fabrics affects emotion in too many ways to discount: sunny versus somber colors; light, airy fabrics versus heavy, opulent fabrics; flowery and romantic fabrics versus tailored, striped fabrics.

Curtains and draperies can cover architectural flaws or enhance beautiful woodwork. They soften edges, contain drafts and provide privacy. Truly, curtains and draperies do it all.

A wide expanse of window is enhanced with a combination of silk valance and draperies.

Matching, with lush trim.

Installed at ceiling level.

Pinch pleat with sheers.

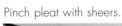

Unique soft cornice caps stationary draperies.

About curtains & draperies

In many homes, it is the fabric window treatment that commands the focal point of the room — far more often than any piece of furniture ever could.

What is it about fabric at the window that makes such a compelling statement? Of course, it can soften the architecture of a room, but it also has the unique ability to accentuate it as well. Fabric can hide flaws around a window area, trap drafts, shield a room's furnishings from the sun and provide a needed focal point.

It can help to muffle sound, manage to pull all the disparate elements of a room together, provide balance and best of all: bestow beauty.

Perhaps you are wondering about the difference between curtains and draperies. It can be confusing, because while curtains and draperies are sometimes similar in appearance, they aren't necessarily similar

in construction. Let me explain.

Curtains are mostly just unlined versions of draperies, a simple single or double layer of fabric that is hemmed and hung from a rod at the top of a window frame. Not all curtains are short but the most recognizable of curtains are those that hit the sill of the window and do not extend to the floor (although some will!).

Curtains can also be defined as a more "novelty" style treatment, probably due to the fact that you will see them used most often in kitchens, bathrooms and children's bedrooms, where fun patterns incorporating various related motifs are pretty standard. So, by nature, they are almost always a less formal style of window enhancement.

Draperies are the grand older sister to curtains, all dressed up and ready for a night on the town. Draperies are for formal areas, areas in need of lush

The room is unified with matching draperies on each window.

accents and also employ complicated stitching and multiple layers.

Draperies are the kind of window treatment that you invest heartily in and expect to keep on the windows for many years.

What is the easiest way to tell a drapery from a curtain?

First, the weight of the fabric. While some draperies can be lightweight, such as if they are made of silk, many will be constructed of heavier materials such as velvet, jacquard, satin, matelassé and damask.

And, if they are made of a lighter material, you will more than likely see that the "beauty" material has been lined at least once, if not twice or even three times.

Lining your draperies provides stability to the beauty fabric, bulks it up and best of all, protects it.

These methods of lining include:

- Interfacing, which is used to support and provide shape to the fabric. It is sometimes stitched directly to the primary fabric but depending upon the selected fabric, it can also be fused with heat. It would be covered with a lining to conceal it, as it is not an attractive product.
- Interlining is also a layer that provides stability and bulk to the treatment, but also pads and stiffens it. Better yet, it is a great insulating layer and keeps light from shining through the treatment, changing its appearance. The interlining is stitched to the back of the primary fabric and finished with a lining layer.
- Lining. All draperies should be lined. This will protect the primary fabric from sun and potential water damage, provide bulk and also offer a kind of "blank slate" look from the street.

Simple rod pocket drapery panel.

Here, draperies run on a track versus hang off of a rod.

There are many, many popular curtain and drapery styles. Here are a short few; you will see even more as you page through this chapter, of course. For curtains, there are:

- Café. Short, cute little curtains that usually only cover about half of the window — enough to offer some privacy but also allow constant sunlight.
- Flat panel curtains are simple fabric panels that have been hemmed on all four sides. They are hung with charming clip-on or sew-on rings.
- Grommeted curtains are flat paneled curtains with the hardware sewn into the top part of the panel. The hanging rod is fed through the grommets and then installed onto the end brackets. Grommets are usually placed close enough within the fabric that by pushing the panel to the side, folds are created. Grommet-top curtains

are usually viewed as a more "modern, edgy" type of curtain because the hardware — almost always metal — is such a focal point.

- Hourglass & stretched (or shirred) curtains are typically used on doors and some windows — but only those windows that you would want an obscured view at all times. Stretched taut from top to bottom and held in place with a rod at the top and bottom, the hourglass is created by cinching the treatment in the middle with either a fabric band or some kind of tie.
- Tab-top & tie-top curtains are just variations of each other. With tab top curtains, the curtain header is a series of tabs that the rod slides through. A tie-top curtain has a set of strings instead of tabs, and they are tied individually onto the rod.

As for draperies, you will possibly appreciate:

Rod pocket stationary panels enhance an alcove.

Formal panels with sheers are capped with a soft cornice and trim.

- Banded draperies define the edge of a drapery panel by using contrast fabric on one or more sides. Banding can occur on the bias — that is, turning the fabric in an opposite direction, such as if a vertically striped treatment had its banding constructed so that the stripes ran horizontally; or perhaps a solid color contrast band on a floral treatment. Banding also adds weight and helps the treatment hang well.

- A flip topper is a contrast lined fabric panel that flips over the top of a rod. The primary fabric shows for most of the treatment, but the contrast lining shows at the top and over. Typically, the flipped area will be styled in some way, such as with tassels or beads, or even cinching or tapering the fabric into a point of sorts.

- The French pleat, also known as a pinch pleat, is a tri-fold pleat at the top of the drapery and is certainly one of the more popular window treatment styles. Held in place like little trios of soldiers, the pleat is then "pinched" at the bottom near the soldier's ankles. Each pleat then balloons out slightly to offer bulk.

- The rod pocket can be found on either curtains or draperies. One reason is because it is such a stable method, with the weight of the treatment evenly distributed. The construction? Easy. The header is folded over to the back and then stitched shut, creating a hollow pocket through which a rod slides.

A few more things

Today, as windows swoop to the ceilings, and even into the ceilings of many homes, fabric at the windows is an important statement. Consider every possibility as you come to a decision.

Draperies of unusual shape are the room's focal point.

Luscious goblet pleated draperies.

Draperies enhance but do not pull focus. This is a gorgeously appointed roomset.

A very wide drapery panel is combined with roman shade.

Swags follow the window arch with accompanying panels.

Bishop sleeves and a swagged soft cornice are an elegant combination.

Sheers under heavier drapes soften the light.

Stationary panels accent a corner area.

Timeless appeal of ring top draperies enhanced with Roman shades.

Incredibly sumptuous, heavy silks with touchable trims.

A true combination of color and style.

A combination of fabrics add depth to this simple flat panel set.

(above) Very sophisticated taupe draperies over sun-filtering sheers.

Stationary panels soften the hard blind treatments.

Ballgown beautiful traversing pinch pleated draperies.

A swag and tail culminate in a lengthy drapery panel.

Bishop sleeves are swagged and draped with fabric shades.

(below) Waterfall draperies tumble down the walls luxuriously.

Simple flat panel attached. Design by Julie Meyer, Interiors by Decorating Den   Mock Bishop's sleeve stationary panel.

Creamy tone-on-tone room with lined draperies to block the morning sun. Simply stunning!

Ceiling level draperies elongate the area.   Daintily edged sheers are crisp looking.

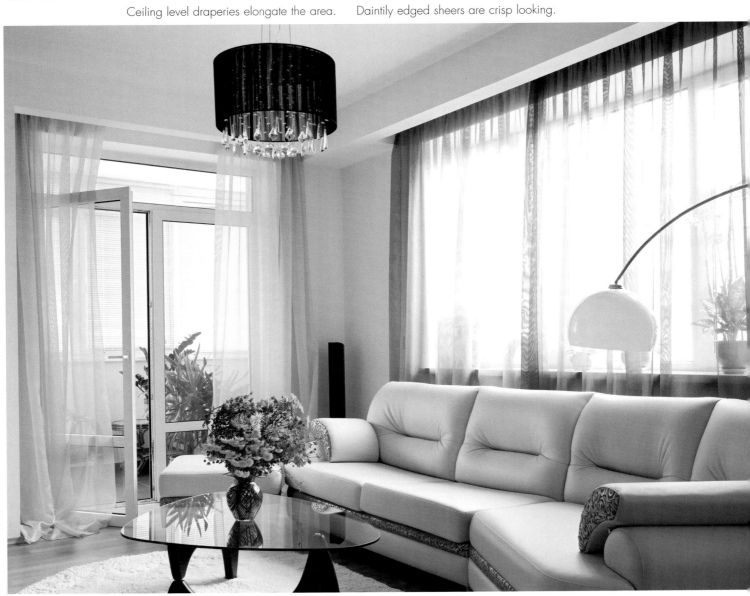

Whisper thin sheers air kiss the floor.

Pinch pleats, tailored and well-constructed.

Fan pleats with banded edge.

A simple traversing panel is enhanced with wood cornice.

Ring top panels provide privacy as well as beauty.

Soft spring tones enhance draperies and soft cornice.

Bold pattern = show stopping draperies.

Yummy florals with bead trim.

Toile patterned draperies accompany a Roman shade.

Subtly patterned sheers take a back seat to the bold tablecloth.

Plaid stationary panels with fringe soften the woodwork.

In the drapery installationa above and below, a track is installed at ceiling level. Panels glide easily to reveal or conceal the view.

(above & below) Traversing drapes lighten the rooms they inhabit.

(above) Stacked at the corner, these draperies take up little space.

Soft sheers recessed into the ceiling.

Sometimes a simple tieback is all that is necessary.

Subtle fabric striping delights.

Tailored beauty.

(below) Silk panels enhance with fresh tones.

Sheer rod top curtains paired with a roller shade.

Clever swing rod allows door access.

Toile drapery panel is echoed in throw pillows. Photo courtesy of Calico Corners

Combination treatment offers privacy and beauty.

Wall of fabric offers sumptuous luxury.

Grommet topped sheers round the corner, creating a wall of fabric, easily moved.

Heavy velvet panels grace the windows as well as upholstery.

Soft fabric panels soften concrete walls.

Taupe and cream tones are soothing.

Modern grommet top splits the focus with contrasting fabric.

Slouchy shabby chic puddling panels.

Two-story sheers run on a motor to open and close.

Subtle grommet top.

Frilly curtains look welcoming.

Panels look stationary but can be released from hold backs.

Dramatic two story draperies.

(above) Wide pleats on a bank of drapes. (below) A winning combination treatment!

(above) Formal panels with sheers. (below) Gorgeous prints attract the eye. *Photo courtesy of Calico Corners*

(above) Sun colors at the window make the room bright, even when the drapes are closed.

Modern sheers tie the room decor together.

Sheer swags enhance silk stationary panels.

A stationary panel is not the best choice for a bedroom.
Hopefully, shades will be installed soon.

Colorful stripes draw the eye.

(below) A panel placed at the ceiling creates instant, eye-catching height.

Blinds

NEAT, COMPACT AND ORDERLY, THE STRUCTURED simplicity of a horizontal or vertical blind offers universal appeal. From magnificent wood blinds that can hold their own in any room, picking up where the moldings have left off for timeless appeal, or a vertical blind system, one of the best for covering a large area such as a sliding glass door or even a simple metallic blind in an eye-catching color, blinds have been a choice in homes throughout the world — for centuries. Note, too the newer hybrid blind/shade combination — basically, these are a combination of blind slats with fabric suspended between for light filtering. You will find those products in both the blind and shade chapters. While these products are much newer (approximately mid-'90s) than traditional blinds, they have captivated homeowners.

Vertical blinds on a wide stretch of glass.

Great for smaller areas.

Simple and elegant.

Privacy and an embrace of the architecture.

Thin swag softens horizontal mini blinds.

About blinds

With their structured simplicity, blinds are universally appealing. They are compact, capable of completely disappearing into a headrail with just the pull of a cord (or not — we'll address that shortly), and are able to fulfill many requirements most people have when looking for a window treatment, including privacy and sun control. Blinds are also available in a variety of styles, colors and sizes.

There are two primary kinds of blinds: horizontal, which draw up and down, and vertical, which draw side to side.

Consisting of a headrail system, louvers or vanes, and a mechanism for adjusting tilt as well as lift and/or draw functions, blinds can also be enhanced with decorative tapes and headrails for added flair.

While the first patent on blinds wasn't registered until 1841, say the word "blinds" and you may envision (in a historical context of course), the Venetian blinds of the 1930s and 1940s: cumbersome two inch wide metal slats hung together with fabric strips that controlled the lift and tilt.

Noisy, cumbersome and by some standards, ugly, they were all about function and had little to do with beauty.

In the 1950s through about mid-1970, metal blinds were all the rage, but with the introduction of lightweight vinyl, sales soared further due to their inexpensive price point.

Blinds have not been without their own set of controversy, however. Among the most unwelcome aspects are death-related pull cord and inner-cord accidents (mostly in small pets and children under the age of three) as well as controversy surrounding

Compact and ideal for an area with high humidity.

hazardous lead levels in vinyl blinds associated with lead poisoning in children in the mid-1990s.

Much has been done to counteract these issues. The composition of vinyl blind material has been changed and all heavy lead blinds were yanked from the market shortly after discovery.

In the case of cord accidents, cordless blinds have been developed, new multi-functional single cord systems have been launched and cord modification kits are also provided free of charge from the Window Coverings Safety Council (windowcoverings.org) for any blind manufactured prior to the year 2000. To note: blinds manufactured today with a looped cord should have a "break away" function that, with pressure, causes the loop to snap apart, thus breaking the "noose."

Blinds are typically crafted from wood, faux wood, metal or vinyl.

Note that the slats can be manufactured in a variety of sizes: from the half-inch micro mini-slat of a horizontal blind, to the large, almost Plantation shutter-size slat of a vertical blind. The biggest difference is this: the smaller the slat, the less light leakage you can expect. The larger the slat, the better view of the out-of-doors when the tilt function is employed.

Also, new "no holes" designs, in which the horizontal slats are strung with cords looping around them rather than through them, offer improved light and privacy control.

Wood blinds are crafted with the highest quality wood available (such as basswood or pine), and are capable of taking a variety of stain colors and paint.

Note that the weight of the finished product means you cannot specify a wood blind in areas

(above) Unobtrusive cellular horizontal puts emphasis on furnishings.

where windows exceed a width of 96". In most cases, this will also mean that multiple blinds (such as a trio of three 32" wide blinds) will be installed into one headrail.

Can you imagine trying to easily lift an eight-foot long solid wood blind with just one pull cord? More than likely, the weight of that blind would cause the cord to snap — not to mention how difficult it could be for those people who lack strength!

If you believe you may not have the wherewithall to operate a window treatment easily, you can also look at motorization. With just the click of a remote or the flip of a switch, a hardwired motor should be able to lift any blind, no matter how heavy. Motorization is also a terrific option if the pull cord is in a hard-to-reach area.

Metal blinds are usually fabricated from six-gauge aluminum slat material. Unlike metal shutters (as mentioned earlier) metal blinds are used in interiors all the time. They are tough, sleek and modern looking and can also withstand plenty of abuse.

Special anti-static coatings make the product easy to clean — and metal blinds are available in a host of bright, vibrant colors, terrific for kids' rooms. And not to worry about pull cord hazards — most aluminum blinds are available cordless. But in any case, never install blinds anywhere near a child's crib or anywhere a child could fall into the blind.

Finally, vinyl or PVC is the least expensive of the blind materials available, though some companies offer decorative texturing, which can raise the price somewhat. With vinyl, louver sizes can range up to about 3.5" in width (for verticals). Two-inch vinyl horizontals are the norm. Lightweight, they are able to span somewhat longer distances without sagging.

A few more things

Because blinds are such a universally capable product, you can find them in precut standard sizes at just about any big box retailer or order them in specialty sizes and colors through a variety of interior design and big box sources.

(above) Cellular verticals wrap the wall beautifully.

Neat and compact — no fuss.

Wood verticals shown are a split draw for French doors.

Good for a wide swath of window.

Cellular vertical is a hybrid of a shade and a blind.

Floor to ceiling. Horizontal blinds with fabric suspension.

Blinds take care of privacy and sun control.

Metal blinds work well with metal bedframe.

Two-inch high gloss black wood blinds.

Blinds can also impart great, classic looks.

(above) Modern living.

Privacy provided by the blinds, sun allowed in above.

Wood blinds, beautiful!

A close up reveals the beauty of the blinds.

Continuous cord lift system allows easy raising.

(below) Simple makes a statement.

The bank of two-inch blinds contribute to the modern appeal of this roomset. Photo courtesy of The Shade Store

Coupled with a soft treatment, these wood blinds provide the privacy, sun control — and beauty.

Wood blinds combine with banded pinch pleats.

Golden wood tones blend well with tableset.

So adaptable to any width!

A bathroom becomes the ultimate escape when the blinds are shut.

Photo courtesy of The Shade Store

Blinds extend all the way to the floor.

Contrast tape is a nice detail.

Top treatments cap the wood blinds with coordinating tape.

Faux wood jumps from bedroom to bath perfectly.

Creating a cozy area with wood.

A sumptuous look.

Two-inch wood blinds with decorative tape offer a sleek, comfortable getaway. Photo courtesy of The Shade Store

(above) Unobstructed viewing when fully raised. (below) Wood blinds with decorative tape.

(above) Verticals work well when the need to cover large glass areas is important.

Leaving the architectural element untreated is a great choice.

Black tape harmonizes with the bedframe.

A bank of horizontal blinds covers an area effectively.

Two-inch faux wood blinds are good for high moisture areas.

(below) Verticals cover a window wall well.

Shades

Alone or as a dramatic accompaniment to another treatment, shades come in all shapes, sizes and materials: soft fabric such as Roman or London fold; the hybrid blind/fabric vane combination; cellular, which resemble blinds due to the crisply folded and easily compacted honeycomb cells; and woven wood and grasses. Such tremendous choices for such a simple and beautiful product! You will be amazed at the variety and scope this particular window treatment offers.

Translucent roller shades transmit light but provide sufficient diffusion to eliminate perception of distinct images — resulting in varying degrees of view-through and privacy.

Roller shade. Photo courtesy of The Shade Store

Roller shade. Photo courtesy of The Shade Store

Roman shade. Photo courtesy of The Shade Store

Flat shade is softened further with drapery panels.

About shades

Shades are not just the simple white vinyl rollers you may have seen hanging in your grandmother's home. Shades are also available in wood, fabric and synthetic materials. And, like curtains and draperies, they can be very tailored — or lush and soft. When categorizing shades, you need to look at them as being available in both "hard" and "soft" materials.

Let's first look at roller shades, the type of "hard" shade most people are familiar with. Roller shades operate on a spring clutch mechanism, which controls the vertical positioning of the product. Roller shades can be had in an almost endless variety of fabrics, from sheer to opaque, polyester to a vinyl/fiberglass blend. Neat and flat, roller shades can be dressed up at the bottom hem with fringe, beads and other passementerie, or left plain.

Roman shades, a very traditional cord-operated shade with overlapping horizontal folds, can be con-

structed not only from fabric, but also a multitude of natural materials such as bamboo, various reeds and grasses. Note that a natural product such as woven wood will require more stacking space in the headrail area than a thinner fabric would.

There are a variety of Roman shade styles from flat fold to waterfall to hobbled, but the concept is the same on all: a series of rings are stitched in multiple vertical columns to the back of the shade and are used to guide lift cords.

In a classic flat fold Roman shade, for example, the lift cord is tied to the bottom ring in each column and then threaded up through the rest of the rings and into a pulley mounted directly above the column. All of the cords are then threaded vertically along the back of the headrail or mounting board and then unite into one pull cord, which runs down the right or left side of the treatment, depending

Flat Roman shades, blackout lined for when napping uninterrupted is of ultimate importance. Photo courtesy of The Shade Store

upon customer specification. Yes, this may sound complicated, but in actuality, it's quite simple.

When the pull cord is operated, the folds pull together in a vertical fashion, collapsing neatly into each other. Roman shades can be either "soft" or "hard" depending upon the material selected.

Pleated shades are crafted from crisp but soft synthetic fabric, and from the side look similar to a zig-zag pattern. The pleats look like horizontal creases when in the down position, which is part of the charm of the product. When pulled up into the headrail, a pleated shade will compact into a neat stack and disappear.

An extensive selection of colors, styles and patterns are available from multiple window covering manufacturers. A "pinched" construction means the shade should not lose its pleated quality. Despite the soft nature of this product, it is considered "hard."

Cousin to the pleated shade is the cellular shade,

a series of honeycomb shapes that can be specified in single, double or triple cells for a variety of insulation choices. They can be specified in sheer, semi-sheer or opaque fabric to offer choices in light control. Look for a pleated tab on the back of each cell, which helps provide shape retention. Different cell shapes are also available, as well as cell sizes.

For both pleated and cellular shades, most quality fabrics used are 100% point bond polyester and have been treated with some kind of stain control, such as Scotchguard. You might also find a softer (but very heavy duty) spunlace polyester material to allow filtered light to enter the room during the day. Cheaper shades will feel thin, stiff and paper-like to the touch. Blackout linings, such as Mylar, are also an option.

One particularly nice feature for both of these products is that they can be cut to fit just about any usually shaped window.

Pirouette shades with low profile header.   Light diffusing pleated shades.

Two more shades, created from fabric, are balloon and Austrian shades. Both shades are similar to Roman shades in that they have a pull-cord mechanism for raising and lowering the fabric; the difference is that the shades have soft "billows" of fabric versus the flatter folds of a Roman shade — and Austrian shades go even one step further than balloon shades in that they also offer vertical shirring at each fold for an even blousier effect. These are, quite obviously, "soft" shades.

Solar shades are a unique product, designed to allow continued viewing of the out of doors, all while blocking over 90% of the sun's heat.

Woven wood shade materials are uniquely textured: comprised of reed, bamboo and various harder grasses, then woven into beautiful multi-colored patterns as well as more sedate single color weaves. Due to the intricate and careful design of the materials, the shade material can flex and fold just like any other material, though, as mentioned earlier, it does require more "space at the top" in side the headrail.

The last type of window treatment product I will mention is a kind of "hybrid" blind/shade product that to date, has no true category name, but is beginning to be called by the first incarnation of the product: the Silhouette. Launched in the early-1990s, the Silhouette suspends traditional fabric vanes (most often seen in blinds) between two sheer fabric facings, to create a "shade" effect. The suspended vanes tilt in the same way as a blind: they can be all the way open, all the way shut or somewhere in between, but the fabric in between the vanes acts as a light filter and diffuser.

You can pull the Silhouette up into the headrail for full and unobstructed viewing, just as you could any shade or blind. Note that this product is also available as a vertical treatment, offering the look of fine draperies, but with the room darkening capabilities of the built-in vanes.

A few more things

So many shades are so beautiful on their own, you may not need to add anything else to your window. However, should you decide on a simple hard shade, consider a top treatment to hide the headrail. While headrails today are nice looking, a top treatment will add a finishing touch.

Luminette shades in combination with cornice and silk panels.

Lightweight bottom up/top down pleated shades.

Waterfall woven wood shades.

Solar shades with matching upholstered cornice.

Fabric/vane combo bridges the gap between blinds and shades.

Graceful, light diffusing Nantucket shades.

Honeycomb shades offer a perfect fit, along with good looks.

Note the combination of vertical and horizontal vanes with dividing drapery panel. Unusual!

Sleek pretty shade in a buttery tone with tassel detailing.

Casual soft shades.   A Roman shade with a half box pleat on each side.

Gorgeous beading enhances the edge of the shade.

Inset shades will lie flat within the window frame.

Thin, relaxed Roman shade.

A window wall is well-covered with Austrian shades. Design by Lynne Lawson, Interiors by Decorating Den

Italian strung shade with unique stiffened cornice. Austrian shade in dining room imparts a formal air.

Austrian shade is installed ceiling level. Should the owner want to use the balcony, the shade could rise above the door frame.

Window Treatments: Shades 113

Woven wood shades can cover large expanses of window with relative ease.

Photo courtesy of Calico Corner

Woven wood shades.

Bottom up/top down shade with contrast banding.

Waterfall woven wood shades.

Woven wood coupled with ring top draperies.

Woven wood shades make a charming statement.

Blackout fabrics are completely opaque, providing advanced light blockage and privacy.

Solar Roman shade.

Solar shades offer a minimal stylish look with practical energy efficient benefits.

Simple and modern — a terrific choice for the windows.

With bountiful interior colors, the subdued striped Roman unifies and balances the room.

White reverse roll solar shade.

Pleated shades are lightweight and thus able to cover a very large expanse of glass with little issue.

Bold balloon shades offer cheery elegance.

Unique Roman shade mirrors arched window.

Whimsical large scale pattern draws the eye.

The fabric shade, accompanying draperies and chair seat covers harbor the same fabric, making this room a special place.

Woven wood shades offer gentle light diffusion.

Silk dupioni tulip Roman shades. Photo courtesy of The Shade Store

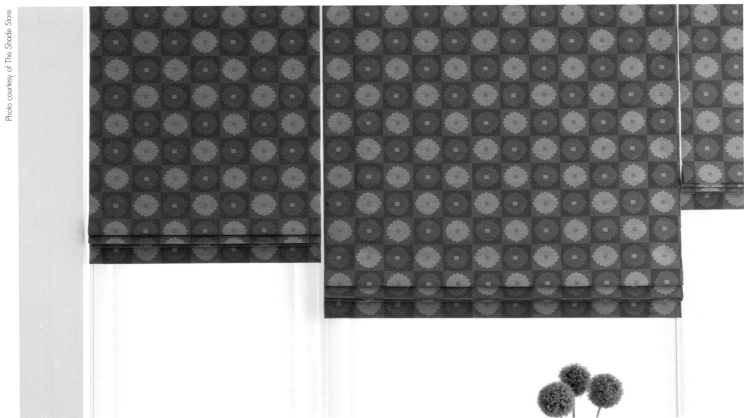

(above) Blackout lined flat Roman shades. (below) Fringe accentuates lovely balloon shades.

Balloon shade fills small alcove efficiently. Photo courtesy of Sarah Barnard Design.

Relaxed Roman shade. Photo courtesy of The Shade Store

Photo courtesy of Sarah Barnard Desin

Whimsical large scale pattern draws the eye.

Top Treatments

SO OFTEN WE LOOK STRAIGHT AHEAD AS WE ENTER A

room, hardly allowing the eye to wander upward. It is

the top treatment that offers a splendid change of

focus, pulling the eye upward with its graceful swaggy

swoops, its carefully placed rosettes and as a wonderful

finishing punctuation to a soft or hard treatment. Plus,

top treatments offer the benefit of beauty in a small

space, so if you wish to have fabric at the window, but

there isn't room for much, the top treatment is a grand

solution. Creative exploration, due to its small scale,

make top treatments a favorite with designers. Look

for clever patterns and colors you might not see on

something full length. Such fun!

Board mounted swags with ball fringe make for a restful,
relaxed alcove.

Crisp floral freeform swag.

Rich fabrics coupled with bullion fringe.

A box pleat valance provides crisp detail.

Simple upholstered cornices hide the drapery hardware for the three sets of stationary panels.

About top treatments

What is a top treatment? The basic definition is that it is a "short" treatment that can stand on its own as a beautiful accent; or can embellish an existing treatment. Top treatments can be fussy and elegant, soft and charming, or even boxy and regimented.

A cornice is a wood frame made to fit across the top of a window, and then is padded and covered with fabric. While the structure of the cornice is quite formidable, the cornice can be anywhere from casual and kitschy to elegant and ornate.

A soft cornice is one in which the padded fabric hangs down below the actual frame, which will allow more movement and whimsy.

Another type of cornice is called the lambrequin, which is basically a cornice with "legs" that extend down on either side of the window frame as an added design element.

Next is the swag, a top treatment that is ever-popular. As with anything wildly popular, the treatment has been over used, constructed poorly and can be found in those dreadful "window treatment in a bag" deals at your local bed and bath store. Stiff and scratchy, almost painful to look at when employed with large-scale florals and garish colors, swags have gotten a bad rap over the years.

However, even the most basic swag treatment, constructed, lined and created with the proper fabric, can be a joy to behold, with its graceful, swooping curves and symmetrical lines. Today, you will find swags in soft fabrics such as sheers and silks, and colors, tiny patterns and reversible linings.

There are a variety of swag styles, and you will see them all as you page through this chapter.

A single swag should be no wider than about three feet — any more than that will make this semi-

Matching swags enhance this already formal room.

circle treatment dip proportionately too low in order to retain its shape or, it will look more like an upside down eyebrow — stretched too thin. At its longest point, swags should reach down into the window no more than 20". Like just about any other window treatment, however, 16" is standard.

There is a term that will come up quite often in conjunction with swags. It's called a "tail" or "jabot." You will commonly hear "swag & tails" — they are often hand-in-hand partners.

The tail is simple decoration, a fabric drop that will accent the beauty of the swag, usually situated on either side of the swag. Do you recall the lambrequin I described earlier? This is the soft fabric version of the legs on the lambrequin.

Sometimes pleated, sometimes gathered (depending on the type of swag, of course), it is a separate piece of material that is installed over or under a board- or pole-mounted swag and will visually balance the treatment.

Most tails will taper to a point and will often be embellished with a tassel or other type of passementerie, such as beads or fringe.

The last top treatment category is valances, and like cornices, the possibilities are endless.

By definition, a valance is a horizontal treatment that fits across the top of a window frame. It can be suspended from a board, much in the way a soft cornice does; or it can hang from a rod. Ranging from complex to entirely simple, the valance can be a treatment all on its own, but also will serve as a beautiful shield to hide cords, headrails and other window treatment hardware, should it be used in combination with, for example, a shade.

As I mentioned, there are many valances limited only by the imagination, but here are a few of the

Tab top valance in popular, warm colors.

Blue and beige tab top valance with button accents.

most popular:

A triangle valance, probably the most simple of the window valances, is similar to tying a handkerchief around ones neck in a jaunty manner. Casual and so simple to make, it is a square of fabric shaped just like a handkerchief, only (obviously) much larger, that is secured to either side of the window frame.

Butterfly and stagecoach valances look like they can be lowered like a shade, because they apppear visually weighty. In both styles, they are "held up" with straps, tabs or whatever you can dream up.

The butterfly valance allows the fabric to spill to each side of the straps, creating what looks like wings. The stagecoach valance cuts straight across with no spill over.

Rod pocket. Yes, here's the old reliable resurfacing in yet another window treatment. So, the drill is the same. The rod-pocket valance is just basically a much shorter version that a curtain or drapery with one difference: it runs the entire length of the rod, versus being divided into two separate panels.

A gathered pick up valance is a beautiful treatment that actually looks a lot fussier than it is. It is

merely a flat, lined, rectangle valance that has had little tucks sewn into the top, which then draws the fabric up into charming little swag-like bells. It is typically lined with a contrasting fabric because, like Mammy flashing her crinoline at Mr. Rhett Butler in *Gone with the Wind*, wherever the fabric is slightly lifted by the tucks, the contrast lining will show.

Pleated valances, such as the ever-popular box pleated valance, are a mainstay of the window treatment business. Crisply tailored or softly gathered, the symmetry of a pleated valance is a welcome addition to any environment.

A few more things

Throughout this chapter, you will see many different types of top treatments. Truly, if you can envision it, it can probably be done. Top treatments are by far the most creative and fun of any of the treatments.

If you want a little fabric at the window, but not too much, the top treatment is definitely the way to proceed.

Box-pleated cornices with gentle arch.

Soft board mounted cornice.

Simple ring top softens the pleated shade.

Swag and jabot mounted cleverly in a bay window.

Window Treatments: Top Treatments

Soft pole mounted swag is enhanced with black reverse.

Design by Leann Robinson, Interiors by Decorating Den

Two-toned swag shows both sides of fabric efficiently.

Classic freeform scarf swag.

Window Treatments: Top Treatments

(above) Blue box pleat valance is the only treatment for this window and its view! (below) Green upholstered cornice spans the window.

(above) Green edged, full valance. (below) Fan pleated top treatment is heavenly with matching cafe curtain.

(above) Tiny balloon valances cap the arch above matching Roman shades.

Board mounted swag and tail hides drapery hardware.

Design by Barbara Tabak, Interiors by Decorating Den

Classic swags and jabots follow the window architecture.

Simple tasseled soft cornice resembles a Roman shade.

Beautiful upholstered cornice with pleating details.

Luxurious board-mounted semi-swag with lush jabot and rosettes, dripping with fringe. Design by Patty Hughes, Interiors by Decorating Den.

Pretty, sheer scarf swag.   A cleverly crafted swag and tail treatment!

Perfectly folded pole mounted swags.

Design by Michelle Davis, Interiors by Decorating Den

A perfect example of pole mounted swag with oversized tail.

Sheer swag with matching sheer draperies.

Swags with rosettes culminate in Bishop sleeve panels.

Remarkable upholstered cornice with accent detailing covers a grand amount of space beautifully.

Trimmed swags and tails accent heavy silk drapery panels.

Pole mounted swags puddle effortlessly.

Pole mounted swags, artistically draped.

(above) Fringe enhances a five fold swag. (below) Unusual decorator valance with tent-flap detailing.

(above) Mock triangle valance. (below) A board mounted swag treatment. Aligning stripes, too, is difficult during construction.

(Above) Box pleated valance with scalloped edge.

Charming awning-style top treatment.

Simple rod pocket top treatment.

Wood cornice enhances architecture and conceals the hardware from the two other treatments.

A simple tab top treatment is nicely paired with horizontal blinds.

(Below) Soft toile print box pleated cornice.

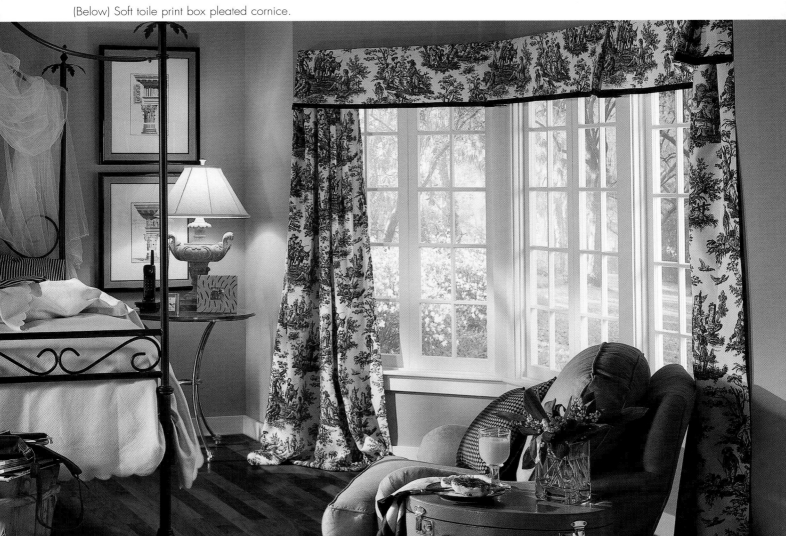

Wall Coverings

APPROACH YOUR WALLS LIKE AN ARTIST TAKING to canvas. There are so many options to express yourself. Wallpaper is back in fashion, as is texture — all the wonderful dimensional qualities that tile, stone and fabric can impart.

Murals in painted and papered form; tile set up as mosaic can bring a feature wall into focus, creating dramatic impact. Plain walls can make art pop in ways one might not expect, vibrantly festive walls crackle with energy and soothing tones of moss, water and wood can calm considerably. Unless you envision a white-on-white room (which can be very sophisticated), add color in a profound way — decorate those horizontal surfaces!

Dramatic wood paneling accented with metal make for a modern living space.

Fabric walls

Fabric walls

Fabric walls

Fabric walls

Fabric walls

Fabric walls

Fabric walls

Painted walls: color wash

Painted walls: combing

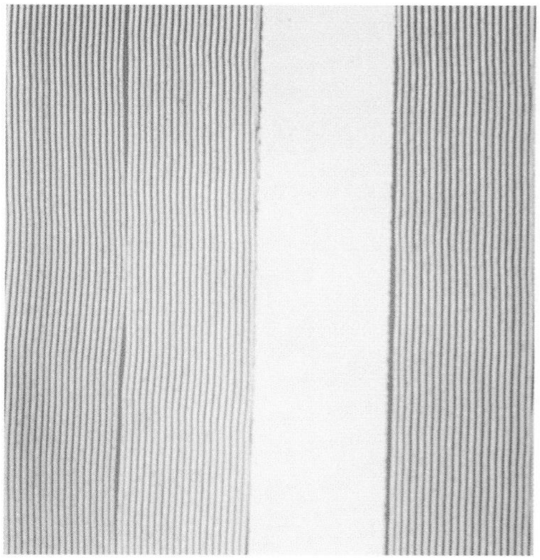

Painted walls: crackle

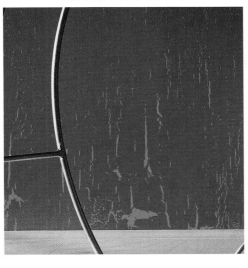

Painted walls: metallic

Painted walls: rag roll

Painted walls: soft suede

Painted walls: sponging

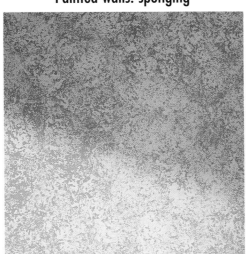

Painted walls: murals

Painted walls: murals

Painted walls: murals

Painted walls: murals

Painted walls: murals

Painted walls

Painted walls

Painted walls

Painted walls

Painted walls

Painted walls

Painted walls

Papered walls

Papered walls

Papered walls

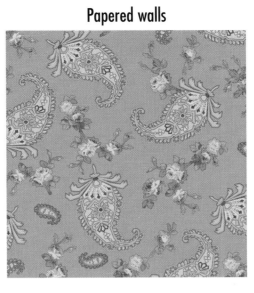

Papered walls

Papered walls

Papered walls: bold

Papered walls: bold

Papered walls: borders

Papered walls: borders

Papered walls: large pattern

Papered walls: large pattern

Papered walls: retro

Papered walls: small pattern

Papered walls: subtle pattern

Papered walls: subtle pattern

Papered walls: stripe

Tile & stone walls

Tile & stone walls

Tile & stone walls

Tile & stone walls

Tile & stone walls

Tile & stone walls

Tile & stone walls

Tile & stone walls

Tile & stone walls: glass

Tile & stone walls: glass

Tile & stone walls: glass

Tile & stone walls

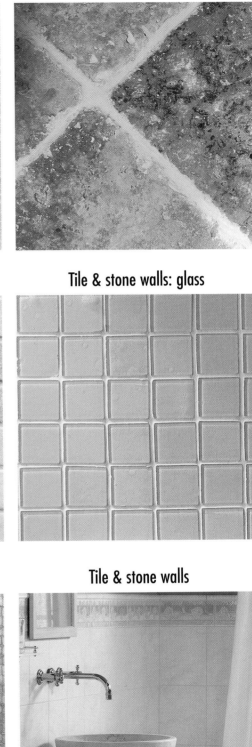

Tile & stone walls

Tile & stone walls

Tile & stone walls

Tile & stone walls

Tile & stone walls

Tile & stone walls: cement

Tile & stone walls: cement

Wood walls

Wood walls

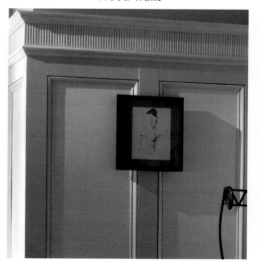

Wood walls

Wood walls

Wood walls

Wood walls

Wood walls

Wood walls

Wood walls: moulding applique

Wood walls: moulding applique

Wood walls: paneled

Fabric

OF ALL THE WALL COVERINGS AVAILABLE, NOTHING SAYS LUXURY like a fabric wall treatment. Soft to the touch, insulating (both temperature and sound), colorful and capable of covering a multitude of wall flaws, fabric can convey an emotional aspect to a room unlike anything else.

Cover a wall entirely with fabric or perhaps just a tapestry will do. Place a drapery rod across a wall and suspend fabric from it, much like a regular curtain or drapery. There are many possibilities explored in this chapter, so why don't you turn the page and learn more?

Imposing upholstered wall brings emphasis to the stately bed ensemble.

Fabric wall behind bed.

Large repeat fabric pattern functions as art.

Tapestry serves to cover walls well.

Divide a space in a new way.

About fabric

Of all the wall coverings available, nothing says luxury like a fabric wall or ceiling treatment. Soft to the touch, insulating (both temperature and sound), colorful and capable of covering a multitude of wall flaws, fabric can convey an emotional aspect in a room unlike nothing else.

For a luxurious feel, drape the fabric in soft folds, stapling and gathering in deep, rich layers. For a more tailored, masculine look, be sure to ask for starched fabric, folded and creased neatly. For an easy installation, consider installing a drapery rod from wall to wall at ceiling level and hanging the fabric from it, much like a simple drapery.

It is probably true that an animal skin over the entrance to a cave was this world's first look at fabric walls and tapestries. A little fast forwarding in our world's history, however, will get us to a more familiar style of fabric wall and ceiling.

The Parthenon in ancient Greece had walls covered with fabric. The Middle Ages saw elaborate tapestries used for dual purposes: to provide privacy as well as insulation from drafts and cold. The oldest existing set of tapestries, woven in Paris between 1375 and 1370, tell the story of the Apocalypse of St. John and reach a length of 471 feet.

By the middle 1600s, the Les Gobelins factory in Paris employed 800 artisans, creating the most sumptuous of tapestries. To own a tapestry was to exhibit a societal rank beyond what most could ever hope to have as decoration in an abode.

Today, a fabric surface is still considered the epitome of high-end. Consider the decoration of the homes of today's "royalty" for example. The White House displays Mrs. Kennedy's lovely green watered silk walls in the Green Room. Buckingham Palace's State Dining Room touts red silk damask. There are lemon yellow damask walls in the Lady Bird Johnson suite at the Grand Hotel on Mackinac Island, Michigan.

As consumers, we see fabric everywhere — but sadly, it is underused in the home as a wall and

Leather insets on wood wall create interest and help absorb sound.

ceiling decoration. It is the fabric padding our commercial work cubicles that most of us are privy to.

So what types of fabric applications can you consider?

For just a small touch of fabric, consider hanging a wall tapestry. Rich with history, the tapestries of medieval times were a beautiful form of artistic expression come to life through weaving. Like a fine painting, a fine piece of tapestry will draw the eye and delight the senses, as well as pull together other colors and textures within a room.

Polished cottons, silk, damask, chintz and other cotton fabrics are the easiest to apply, due to their pliability. Note, too, that fabric is easier to handle than wallpaper because it is not stiff nor will it tear easily. And while starch is messy, fabric goes onto the wall dry, so there is no booking time or long, wet strips of paper to create havoc.

Consider hanging a drapery rod from wall to wall and either hanging fabric from the rod or draping it over. Remember, however, that the rod will need to be braced about every two feet for maximum strength, which may interfere with your end result.

In general, a fabric draped ceiling is more of a cosmetic fix or an enhancer than a true, installed ceiling. Typically, fabric is draped to cover an unsightly or damaged ceiling rather than to function as an actual ceiling. But beauty is the end result!

When purchasing fabric, remember that the more draping and shirring you desire, the more fabric you will need. For example, should you decide to shirr your wall with small pleats, you will need to purchase about two times the wall width. Also consider any accent pieces you may want to create or cover, such as accent pillows, bedskirts or window treatments. It's always best to purchase the fabric all at once (such as with wallpaper) so you are working within the same dye lot.

Understand, too, that the fabric weight (a heavy, hard to conform fabric, versus a lighter cotton), will impart a mood as well. Of course, some fabrics work better for use on a wall than others. The more diffi-

Interesting use of stiffened fabric is visually unique.

Tropical flair moves from wall to window.

Covering a wall with a large tapestry is a great way to introduce fabric without the fuss of installation. Design by Suzanne Price, Interiors by Decorating Den

cult the fabric is to fold and manipulate, the more difficult your installation will be. And, don't be intimidated with the "cleaning" aspect. Vacuuming works well.

For those of you who rent, or have a hard time making a decision that involves installing something permanent on a wall, consider hanging fabric instead. Say goodbye to white walls in a rented apartment, for example, by hanging a large tapestry or by draping a large piece of fabric behind a sofa.

Instead of padding the walls with batting, you can also choose to adhere fabric directly to the wall with starch. Use a regular paint roller to roll liquid starch onto your surface. Take your cut piece of fabric (about six inches longer than you need — you will overlap at the floor and ceiling), and smooth the fabric onto the wall.

After you are certain it is straight and adhering well, use your paint roller again over the fabric, saturating it with starch. With your next piece of fabric, be sure to turn your abutting seam over and layer it over the raw seam of the first strip of fabric. This will create a neat seam and keep fabric from unraveling.

A few more things

Yes, fabric can be intimidating, but if you are interested in an unusual wall treatment, certainly something that not any home boas, then consider fabric for your next decorating project.

Draped behind a bed.   Window and wall covering made of identical fabric.

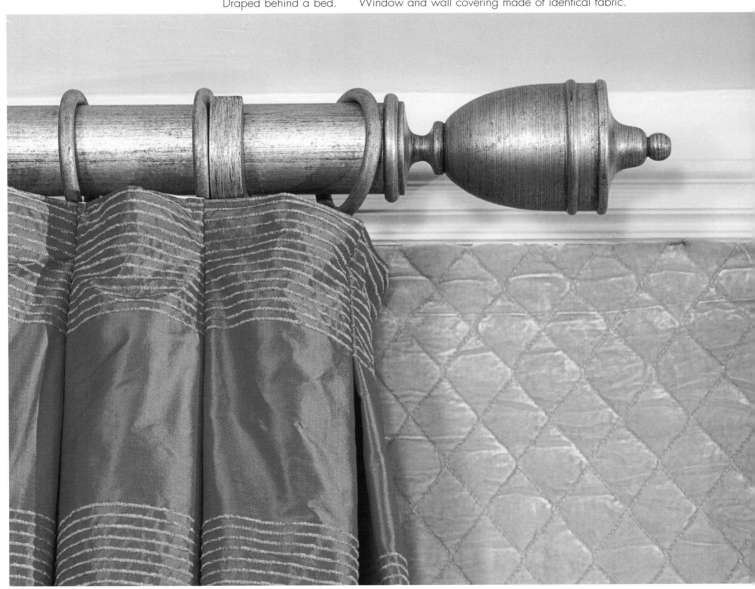

Upholstered wall.

Fabric moves from wall to corona.

Dainty wall fabric is a great foil for the larger scale pattern on the bed.

Fabric on the wall is from the same collection as the draperies.

Tapestry breaks up the color of the walls, creating interest.

Billowing fabric hangs from two rods placed on the ceiling.

Creating a cozy nook with a drapery-style fabric wall.

Tapestry hung ceiling level offers a soft artistic element.

Large tapestry covers wall entirely.

Picking up the color tones from the wall with fabric.

Fabric covered room divider.

A long stretch of fabric can cover any wall problem.

Paint

IT IS WELL KNOWN THAT RESPONSE TO color can vary from human to human, age group to age group, sex to sex. Mostly, it is because human emotions are not stable and are hard to measure scientifically. Emotions change depending upon numerous uncontrollable stimuli, including hormone levels, environment, health ... the list could continue for quite some length. But there are some givens: warm colors (red, yellow) make most people feel active and alive, and cool colors (blue, green) subdue and harken to the environment. Additionally, light colors imply or make people feel more alert and aggressive; dark colors, more somber and passive.

Colors mean different things to different cultures, too, making the analysis of color response even trickier.

When you choose a paint color for your room, don't stick entirely to what's in style, what's popular — but what you find attractive and fulfilling to your design ideal.

Sky blue ceiling with tan walls complements bedding.

Bright tropical blue perks up a kitchen.

Faux wallpaper. I.e..; paint.

Rust and gold makes for an exotic bedroom.

Sandy brown tones with white accent moldings is clean and neat.

Beige coupled with textured wallpaper — a great combination.

Coffee with cream coloration coupled with light blue.

About paint

One can look to the cave paintings of the Upper Paleolithic era, nearly 40,000 years ago, executed with materials such as charcoal, ochre and hematite, as the seed of the paint industry as we know it today. Ancient painted walls in Egypt, some 2000 years ago, still exhibit brilliant color, quite possibly due to a gummy, resilient binder they used when mixing them. However, their method of mixing colors was more of a layering process, one pure color over another pure color, without blending.

Fast forward to the late 1800s, when the first washable paint, Charleton White, was introduced. It wasn't until the Industrial Revolution, however, that paint became recognized in the U.S. as a viable economic-enhancing commodity.

Today, a host of latex, environmentally-friendly and low VOC paint and finish products rule our roosts, with sales in the billions of dollars yearly. Paint made from clay, bees wax, mineral dye, milk protein and more offer pleasant citrus fragrances while drying — or some have no fragrance whatsoever.

There are two basic types of "finish" paint products available: oil or latex, and four types of "sheen" available: gloss, semi-gloss, flat and satin.

Latex is by far the most popular due to its ease of use. Both products, however, have four components: water, pigment, binder and additives.

Latex is a simple paint to employ, as it cleans up with soap and water, dries quickly, and is less odor-

Blues and creams are a welcoming combination.

Photograph courtesy of Interiors by Decorating Den

Rich browns and rust make up a beauty of a sitting area.

ous. Also, is it less apt to blister, peel and crack because it allows moisture to evaporate through its surface. The best types of latex paints are comprised of 100% vinyl/acrylic resin and very little liquid. Less expensive latex paints contain more water and thus are less effective because the coverage is less dense. This can also mean that it will be more prone to fading and less resistant to dirt and stains.

Also consider that you may end up spending more time and money using cheaper paint, being you may have to apply two coats, versus the one you would need with a higher quality, thicker paint.

Oil paint, also known as alkyd, contains a strong binder made from vegetable oil and is best used in areas of high wear, such as door trim or cabinets, as it dries to a hard finish. The binder makes this type of paint difficult to clean up. A solvent, such as mineral spirits, is needed to clean painting equipment and spills.

In regard to sheen levels, you will need to consider how much surface wear you expect to encounter.

Flat paint offers a matte finish, which is good for hiding surface imperfections. It also absorbs light well and is typically used on ceilings and areas where cleaning is not an issue. Flat paint is for areas of light use, as it is not very durable.

Satin paint provides a soft, subtle sheen, similar to the shell of an egg. Also known as an eggshell, pearl or velvet finish, it is a good choice for areas with more use, such as hallways, children's rooms and stairways.

Note how the blues and browns of this interior co-mingle.

Light green and lavendar — a classic combination.

Semi-gloss is a durable paint with high stain resistance, used primarily on wood trim or in rooms requiring some wall scrubbing, such as a bathroom or kitchen. It will draw attention due to its glossy appearance, which can be a drawback, as surface blemishes can be more visible. Semi-gloss can be a good base coat for elaborately painted finishes, such as marbeling.

For areas that take a daily beating, such as a stairway banister, painted furniture, cabinets, steps and some areas of the kitchen, you can't beat the gloss finish. It is good to note that the high gloss, while easy to scrub also displays surface imperfections, like nicks or scratches, more readily. Use gloss for a very slick, attention-capturing look. Gloss is not appropriate for walls, unless it is an area that will need repeated cleaning.

A few more things

Paint is inexpensive and easy to change out. Easy to apply, easy to clean up, paint is a quick change artist that can provide a new look for a little bit of elbow grease and just as little money. Many paint compa-nies offer small test packages that cover about a 3 by 3 foot section of wall, making it easy to "test drive" a color before you make the commitment to purchase multiple gallons.

Paint won't always cover wall flaws and may also need multiple coats to achieve the color and coverage necessary to conceal the previous wall color. Color can fade due to environmental issues like sun exposure or smoke, thus, touch ups after a certain amount of time are bound to appear subtly different.

Paint colors range from subtle and muted to vibrant and glorious. Here is a quick overview of how color affects mood:

> Brown: earthy, secure, peaceful
> Blue: fresh, peaceful, clarifying
> Gray: discouraging, solid, wise
> Pink: youthful, feminine, flighty
> Beige: quiet, boring, balancing;
> Red: passionate, energetic, attention-grabbing
> Purple: rich, royal, headstrong
> Yellow: optimistic, happy, jarring
> Black: sophisticated, powerful, mysterious
> White: healthy, clean, fresh

(above) Pink and green: a perennial favorite.

Paint wood instead of leaving it natural or staining it.

Green harmonizes well with natural cabinetry.

Green with brown accents are a favorite.

Green and beige pop against white woodwork.

A classic Country French motif with yellow as the backdrop.

Cheerful yellows are a great choice for baby's first room.

Dressing room/bath captivates in pink.

Paint the lighter color first, wait until completely dry, then mask off your area well. Paint the second color. Success!

An inspired color choice!

Olive and teal complement the reclaimed heart pine flooring.

White pops against teal.

Warm tones harmonize.

Dark vivid blue is a complement to natural beech floor.

Green/gray exhibits sophistication.

(above) The compelling colors of the Southwest. (below) Note how sunlight will change your color throughout the day.

(above) Golden wheat tones with blue and stellar woodwork. (below) Complementary wall color lets floor take center stage.

(above) Olive green is the perfect foil for window treatments. Design by Ragan Corliss, Interiors by Decorating Den

Blood red walls are a gamble that paid off well.

Bright red popping behind white is ultramodern.

Dark beige is a soothing backdrop for murky orange.   Tomato red with white and beige.

(below) Captivating colorations move the eye from room to room. Design by Becky Zimmerman, Interiors by Decorating Den

The accessories pop against a subtle wall tone.

Deep, dark chocolate is the focal point as walls recede.

Shades of brown make for sophisticated elegance.

Design by Suzanne Christie, Interiors by Decorating Den

Photo courtesy of Interiors by Decorating Den

A restful place to relax.   Rich milk chocolate tones make for a luxury retreat.

Beige mixed with warm browns and green unite this interior beautifully.

Unusual wall decoration pops against a complementary color.
Design by the team of Hammersley/Bazay, Interiors by Decorating Den

Blood red and gold are visually stunning together.

A dramatic combination of rust and gold.

Design by Ali Maricle, Interiors by Decorating Den

Neutral walls offer a subtle backdrop to the furnishings.

Design by Heather & Jon Pantel, Interiors by Decorating Den

Rag rolled walls show color variance beautifully.

Blue and cream — so inviting. Design by Virginia Smith, Interiors by Decorating Den

Exceptionally clean and modern, not bold.   Purple is a refreshing change in an area of relaxation.

Light lavender/blue walls are a cool foil to natural furniture

Shades of blue make for a restful night.

Blue and yellow is a traditional choice in a guest bedroom.

A palette designed with serenity in mind.

(above) Draperies provide the drama; wall color provides the backdrop. (below) Cheery yellow is so inviting.

Design by Connie Thompson, Interiors by Decorating Den

(above) Furniture symmetry with yellow as the grounding element. (below) Blue pops against yellow.

(above) Complexion pink is a warmer tone that will help the room move from baby to teenager with ease.

The yellow submarine evokes a Beatles album cover.

Purple, blue and green are calming yet also invigorating.

It's always summer in when the walls tout flowers.

Bunnies cavort in a whimsical wall pictorial.

(below) An unusual choice for a bedroom, but the green works well in this application. Design by Chris Sapienza, Interiors by Decorating Den

Wallpaper

After years of being upstaged by neutral backgrounds and faux paint finishes, wallpaper is forging a very successful comeback. Beautiful, vibrant and very, very trendy, wallpaper is the sexiest decorating star of the moment — easier to install than ever with options, textures, sizes and color combinations for every budget and taste.

A cleverly applied paper can make a smaller room look spacious, make a dark room appear light and airy, or a light-filled room seem cozy and intimate. Vertical stripes will elongate an interior; horizontal stripes can make it appear wider. And consider children: it has been noted that the use of pattern — especially repetition in pattern — in a childs' room provides a sense of stability and reinforces problem solving skills.

Unusual, fresh colors for the sitting area keep life lively.

Restrained, warm florals.

Coordinating border is a finishing touch.

Harlequin patterning.

Bold patterns capture attention.

Subtle patterns harmonize well with the decor.

About wallpaper

So, we just covered a big topic, paint. Who would have thought a bucket and a brush had so much possibility? Well, batten down the hatches, because our next category, wallpaper, is beautiful, but misunderstood, and, might I even say, terribly neglected as a design possibility.

You may not have realized this, but wallpaper has been around for almost 600 years, though paper itself was invented over 2000 years ago.

For a while, civilization was content with using paper for its invented purpose: for the recording of ideas, thoughts and art. But in 1481, French King Louis XI commissioned artist Jean Bourdichon to create 50 rolls of painted paper adorned with angels on a blue background. It was then that wallpaper, as we know it, emerged.

In the burgeoning 1700s, Jean-Michel Papillon designed repeats into his paper patterns; later in that century, in America, the oddly-named Plunkett Fleeson began printing wallpaper in Philadelphia.

Today, after suffering through recent decades of neutrally painted surfaces and faux paint finishes, wallpaper is drawing in both young and old alike with its wide range of possibilities, capable of satisfying any decorating urge. Prints are back in fashion, with influences coming from flowers and leaves, and bold, graphic retro motifs are snowballing as well.

And consider texture — something that paint has difficulty replicating. There is a new dimensional quality to wallpaper that adds a sense of depth and interest to a room, unlike any other design element.

There is simulated wood grain — and real wood veneer wallpaper. There is wallpaper that resembles brick, stucco and stone. There is cork wallcovering. Wallpaper has can be infused with mother of pearl;

Rich, gold with subtle patterning delights.

Masculine colors and print, great for the office.

metallic wallpaper shines and draws attention. For commercial usage, there is paper that has been coated with zinc oxide nanoparticles, giving it an anti-bacterial surface — perfect for hospitals.

Finally, wallpaper murals are a means to bring a feature wall into focus, creating dramatic impact in any room. These are easy to install, durable and ultimately more affordable than commissioning a hand painted mural.

Look at the images on this page above the text. Note how subtle the wallcovering images are. Now, look at the previous page. Big and bold, correct? How might these styles translate to your own interior? Can you visualize?

Some people are of the opinion that once wallpaper has been installed, the room cannot be adjusted to changing styles or moods. This depends on the color and pattern selected. Yes, a bold, large-scale pat-

tern may make itself known in a more dramatic fashion. But subtle designs such as Strie, a delicate tone-on-tone striped pattern; Damask, an elegant paper with arabesque scrolling; or the popular contrasting stripe can adapt quite well. For motif designs, choose florals, tropicals, Oriental motifs or toile patterns.

A cleverly applied paper can make a smaller room feel spacious, make a dark room appear light and airy, or a light-filled room seem cozy and intimate. Vertical stripes will elongate an interior; horizontal stripes can make it appear wider. And consider children: it has been noted that the use of pattern — especially repetition in pattern — in a child's room provides a sense of stability and reinforces problem solving skills.

A word about adhesives: wallpaper gained quite the reputation for being difficult when paste needed to be applied by hand onto the wall and onto the

A whirl of large-pattern florals makes for an unforgettable decor.

paper. What a mess! True, some papers still need paste for application, but the majority of papers created today are pre-pasted, which means that they only need a quick dip in a tray of water and a short time period to "book" the paper (this gives the paste time to activate and also allows the paper to expand prior to installation) before it can be hung.

Yes, the process is still somewhat "drippy" and yes, there can be some close encounters with sticky paper, but the end result is magnificent.

Wallpaper is great for masking small dents in wallboard, and can cover up an ugly paint job in a snap. Note that if you are installing light-toned wallpaper over a very dark wall, you may need to either prime the wall in a lighter color, or install "liner" paper — basically the paper equivalent of a primer coat. This will ensure there is no color bleed-through.

A few more things

Wallpaper does have its drawbacks — rips are hard to repair, bubbles will sometimes form under the paper if it hasn't been hung just right, and it takes care to match patterns. You will probably need to purchase more "coverage" than you'll really use, in order to match patterns. One tip: choose a random pattern instead of a pattern you will need to carefully match, to avoid overspending.

Whatever paper you select, based on client specifications, know that the allure of wallpaper lies in the depth, emotion and intensity it brings to a room.

Historical wall treatments harken to a past era.

Dramatic, historical patterning.

Compelling patterning for a dramatic look.

Subdued, rich colors with big but subtle patterning.

Quiet striping adds implied height to the area.

Buddha paper sets a mood of restfulness.

Beautiful floral detailing keeps the eye moving.

Charming floral in muted tones.

(above) Delicate wallpaper detailing and coloration offers a luxurious setting.

Cheery florals are forever inviting.

Rich wallcovering coordinates with fabric treatments.

The large print balances with coordinating fabrics.

Tasteful gold and brown in subtle patterning.

(below) Bold large-scale pattern coordinates with fabric treatments to great effect.

(above) Embossed tone-on-tone wallcovering with hearts.

Captivating paisley-style print.

Breezy, carefree sailboats in a bath area.

Multiple patterns draw the eye.

Cute stripes and teacup bordering for the kitchen.

(below) Modern floral looks fresh and appealing.

Embossed look captures a tin ceiling appearance.

Red and gold always fascinates.

Intriguing wallcovering mural pulls the eye up.
Design by Courtney Willard, Interiors by Decorating Den

Bamboo-look wallcovering in golds and beige.

Black and white florals.

Leafy greens in a black and white twist.

Clean, interesting toile.

Sharp contrasts make black florals pop.

Mod florals entrance with retro style.

Elaborate patterning, easy to achieve with wallpaper.

(above) Brown and mint tones, ever popular. (below) Deco-style paper aligns perfectly with stair risers.

(above) Rosy floral circular pattern creates enhanting movement. (below) A perfect partner, combined with paint.

(above) Textured look adds masculine flair. Design by Shelly Rodner, Interiors by Decorating Den

Textured bamboo motif.

Small pattern adds delicate detailing.

Glossy sheen in a tone-on-tone paper.

Large scale pattern commands the room.

(below) A mesmerizing but overall subtle pattern.

(above) The timeless look of blue and beige.

Large floral print. Note the layered patterning, squares behind the grasses.

Playful purse and hat pattern makes for a fun environment.

Lovely patterns move from walls to linens.

(below) Restrained and elegant, mottled colors entrance. Note contrast pattern in adjacent bathroom. A good use of color continuity.

Rosy-toned *fleur de lis* dot a bright yellow background.

Ribbons of white coil up and down a warm, yellow background.

Various gold seashell motifs capture attention. Note contrast star paper on the ceiling — a nice touch.

Elaborate honeycomb patterning keeps the eye moving.

Subtle stripes mix with swirls.

Rosy-toned and subtle blue stripes.

Faint floral patterning offers soothing backdrop in the bedroom.

Pretty salmon tone — a color not used often enough!

Appealing large-scale floral.

A sumptuous look in a dressing room, tan and pink always delight.

(above) Vibrant checkerboard with inset accent. (below) Attractive modern floral, fun for a teenager!

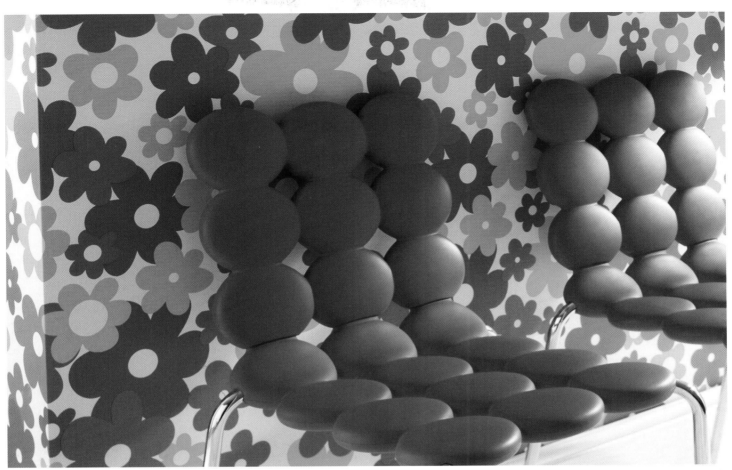

(above) Powerful flowers pop with '60s cool. (below) A very feminine look.

(above) Blue and white — always a favorite. Design by Connie Thompson, Interiors by Decorating Den

Multiple patterns with stripes and florals.

Long grass pattern creates vertical interest.

Tone-on-tone blue floral.

Large scale patterns are always popular.

(below) Color blocks pop!

Tile & Stone

AN EXTRAORDINARY DESIGN TOOL, TILE CAN BE found in any number of shapes, sizes and materials. You will find tile glazed and unglazed, in natural materials such as clay and stone, in manufactured squares, such as porcelain and ceramic, and in sheets, such as glass.

What can be confusing to some is that certain tile types are not suitable for every application. For example, one needs to take a great deal more into consideration when selecting tile for the floor than for a wall, primarily due to wear and safety issues.

For walls, just about anything will do, making the art of wall decoration all that more spectacular with unlimited possibilities for expression.

Rectangular tiles set vertically.

Tile moves from bathroom to bedroom.

Large and small wall tile.

Tri-color blue variations.

Random colorations as well as occasional patterned tiles exhibit beauty.

Natural stone tile.

About tile & stone walls

Tile and Stone is a hardwearing, enduring material, falling under the category of masonry.

What is masonry? Well, the word can describe two related things — both the material used, as well as the actual construction, using those materials. Beyond rough and cut stone and ceramic tile, masonry materials include brick, plaster and stucco, and various forms of concrete.

What's the common thread? Masonry is quite strong and can do anything from decorate an interior as well as protect an exterior. Walls can be built, showers can be decorated, paths can be lined and counter tops can be poured — all using materials from the masonry group.

But let's get back to what you are probably most interested in. Tile and stone.

What can be confusing to some is that certain tile types are not suitable for every application. For example, one needs to take a great deal more into consideration when selecting tile for the floor than for a wall, primarily due to wear and safety issues. We'll talk about tile for floors in a later chapter.

For walls, just about anything will do, making the art of wall decoration all that more spectacular, with unlimited possibilities for expression.

So, where might you use tile or stone? Mostly in bathrooms, in the kitchen as decoration above a countertop or in the entryway. Those areas that need a hardwearing product that also can handle water.

Tile is pretty much a shoo-in for the bathroom area, don't you think? Because when you consider other products to choose for a shower stall, for example — you will want something that can handle the

Captivating colorations in a kitchen installation.

Tiles set diagonally with small bronze flower details.

water. Paint over wallboard won't do it. Neither will wallpaper. Fabric? Don't even think about it. When it comes to an area that is receiving a big dose of water on a daily basis, your first and only thought should be tile, stone or some other impermeable wall material.

Yes, there are other potential products for a shower area. Metal would be one. Glass, too. But 90 percent of the time — most people want tile or stone.

Tile is not just available in squares and slabs of varying sizes, but also in a variety of trim shapes and sizes that will accommodate just about any horizontal or vertical area. Some product lines won't offer as much in the way of functional trim as others; so make certain you note of all design specifications before you choose the product.

There are four categories of tile, which are based upon the level of vitrification. What's vitrification? In layman's terms, it means to change or make into glass or a glassy substance, especially through heat fusion. Now, vitrification as a method of creation can be applied to more than just tile. But with tile, it's all about water absorption rate.

The four categories are Nonvitreous, Semivitreous, Vitreous and Impervious.

The water absorption rate will determine how the tile is used — be it outside, in a wet or high-traffic condition, in hot or cold climates. To make it simple, the nonvitrious tile has the highest water absorption rate, making it prone to stains, cracking and chipping and at the other end of the scale, Impervious tile, as you can probably imagine from its name, has an extremely low water absorption rate and is appropriate for just about any application,

Random color accents keep the eye moving.

including being frost proof. Vitrification is determined in this manner: A dry tile is weighed, then soaked in water, then weighed again. The before-and-after difference in weight is what determines the percentage of water absorbed.

This is important information for you to keep in mind when you are specifying a tile. Will it be indoors or out? Will it be subjected to water?

Another decision you will need to make is in regard to tile color. There are four different color variations: V1, V2, V3 and V4. The "V" stands for variation. Here's an easy way to remember it.

V1 is considered a uniform appearance. That is, if you were to buy a box of tile, and you pulled one piece after the other out of the box, and they would all look the same. No color variance. One color. V1.

V2 is considered having slight variation, which means that there might be a mottled quality to some of the tiles that complements the other. That is, the while the tile color is consistent, the pattern or texture may change somewhat. V2 usually is two colors.

V3 is considered to have moderate variation. This may be a case where you open that box of tile and you pull out three different colors but they all look terrific together. One tile might be 100% brown, the next is 75% brown and the last one is very light — maybe just 25% brown. All the same color, but different and distinct variations of it. Three colors. V3.

Finally, a V4 color palette will be a random variation. Think about painting the exterior of your home, for example. You might have a primary teal blue on the shakes, but then you decide to paint the door a deep forest green and then trim the windows with a café latte brown. This is what you might also find in a set of V4 tile. Random colors — but they all harmonize well.

Does this all make sense?

Let's talk now about the tile names you may be more familiar with. Porcelain probably rang a bell for you. What else might you know? Marble? Yes, that can be tile, but that's stone tile. There's a difference.

What else? Ceramic? Yes, it's a type of tile, though the term is somewhat loose, as a number of types are grouped into this name. There is also quarry tile,

Glass wall serves as a perfect room divider.

Charming, rustic kitchen area.

agglomerate tile and terracotta.

Quarry tiles are made from the same type of material as bricks — clay and also shale. They can include pavers for a walkway or driveway or any other area where a hard-wearing product is needed. This category can include wall, mosaic and floor tile. It can be glazed or unglazed (just as any other tile can be).

Porcelain tiles or pavers are made from pressed dust, which results in a finely-grained, velvet like composition. Where do you think the phrase "porcelain skin" came from? Yes, porcelain is very smooth. But it's also very hard. The fine grains, compressed until solid, allow no room for air. Highly water resistant, it is very difficult to cut and install.

Ceramic tile is clay and other organic materials pressed into a mold, rather than extruded, and then finished in a kiln — a very hot oven of sorts in which a controlled temperature is produced. The material is "fired" until all elements in the mold have merged into one hard piece.

There is one other tile I should mention. Glass.

Tile medallion focuses attention.

Design by Joanne Watson, Interiors by Decorating Den

Natural stone on floor and up the steps — magnificent!

Larger and smaller patterns are an effective installation.

Note three different tile patterns, floor, steps and wall.

Think about it in this way: glass tile, formed through vitrification. Do you think it would stand up well to water? Of course. Glass is non-porous and actually as hard as marble, one of the most dense of the tile products but is less expensive and well-known for its clear color beauty.

A few more things

Stone tile types include granite, limestone, marble, sandstone, slate, and travertine. If you have interest on how these various rocks were formed within the earth's surface, you will need to do some extra reading. I think your eyes would probably glaze over if I started to talk about igneous versus sedimentary formations. However, what we should discuss is how these rocks vary in appearance.

Granite is very distinctive, because it looks as if it has flecks within it. And actually, it does. If you were to analyze a piece of granite, you might find flecks of mica, quartz and feldspar within. Granite is the hardest and most resilient of the stones and suitable for heavy traffic because most scratches or nicks can be buffed out. Granite tones can range from black and white to brown, yellow, pink and blue.

A favorite stone among architects, limestone offers a natural beauty and weathers well. Note that many ancient stone structures standing today are made of limestone and you will understand the appeal. Beauty plus durability. One aspect to consider is that limestone does not hold up well to acids or caustic chemicals. In fact, acid rain has caused problems with architecture. For interiors, however, its

Incredible stone wall pulls all of the attention.

A unusual natural tile.

Rectangular tiles in graduated shades.

smooth, granular surface coupled with light coloration is a knockout choice.

When you think about marble, what kind of adjectives come to mind? Beauty? Luxuriousness? Strength? You would be right on all accounts. With a variety of colors ranging from gray, green or pink to more neutral white and browns, marble offers a wide range of possibility. However, highly polished marble is slippery and will show scratching and staining.

Like limestone, sandstone is a sedimentary rock, and is formed through compression. In fact, you will see that sandstone is layered. Varying in color from white to yellow, pink, red, copper and gray, sandstone can be identified, even, by region. Sandstone will hold up well to heavy traffic.

Hard and quite dense, slate is compact and resist-

ant to stains. With a wide color range including red, green, black and gray, slate reflects heat rather than absorbs it, making it a great choice for cool climates. A smooth stone, it is also brittle and requires care when installing.

Travertine has a unique appearance in that it displays indentations and cavities caused by gas and sulfur rising to the surface when the rock was forming. Because of these craters, cleaning this product is more time consuming. Consider finishing the product with a clear epoxy so that the beauty of the stone shows, but the cavities are closed up so as to not capture dirt.

Colorful, tactile, and the one material able to actually form shapes and tell stories, tile is an exciting, exacting medium.

Photo courtesy of Interiors by Decorating Den

Pearlescent tiles exhibit purples and blues.

Round glass pebble tile in water colors.

High polish cobalt blue tiles make woodwork pop.

Grays, blues and purples offset the woodwork.

Highly artistic floor to ceiling tile installation.

Tile installed floor to wall and above is stunning.

White tile in brick style.

Accent tiles placed in random patterns add focus.

Blue racing stripes pop and add movement.

Glass block coupled with tile.   Beige with black racing stripe accent.

Beautiful blue tile, an eternally popular color.

Vibrant red makes for an inspired color choice.

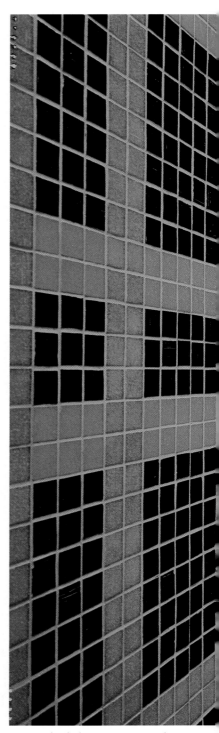

Tartan plaid tile — so eye-catching.

Mosaic makes bathroom a work of art.

Design by Lynne Lawson, Interiors by Decorating Den

Warmth from stone and fire.

Sleek and entirely sophisticated.

Black speckled tile with metallic accent.

Stones of varying shapes create a rustic hearth.

An eye-catching combination of patterns and colors.

A dazzling pattern of movement.

(above) Modern looks. (below) A great choice for moisture-laden areas.

Photo by Toby Ponnay

Photo by Toby Ponnay

(above) Cement and leather for a luuxurious experience. (below) Cement softened with fabric.

Photo by Toby Ponnay

A luxurious retreat exhibiting small and large tile.

Surround and windows in glass block.

Glass block tile divides one private area from the other.

Glass block is a perfect foil for lovely woodwork.

Gradient coloration works effectively to raise the eye up.

No need for a window treatment when glass is mottled.

Cool beige invites.   Decorative patterning creates a focal point.

Distinctive stripes add movement.

Warm earth tones look terrific. Great shabby chic style with brick-shaped tile.

Cool tone-on-tone banding deliver emphasis.

A variety of patterns creates an interesting space.

Warm coffee tones.

A variety of colors, shapes and patterns.

Small tiles mix with larger to create interest.

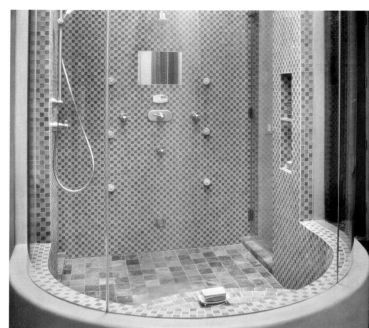
Intriguing water-tone shower stall.

Tiled fireplace matches floor and countertop.

Ceramic backsplash with charming frog motif.

Opalescent water-color tiles are a perfect choice in the bathroom.

Fluted marble in multi-color swirl creates sense of movement.

Motif above stove is an eye-catcher.

(above) Terrific texturing makes for an unusual look. (below) Unbelievable artistry with tile.

(above) An imposing stack, layer upon layer. (below) Brick looks refreshingly new and hip.

Stone fireplace.

Brick walls in mottled gray tones.

Brick painted brown imparts a cozy feeling.

Creating a rustic look with natural stone.

Warm yellow-toned brick.

Stone fireplace reaches to the ceiling to dramatic effect.

Wood

WOOD WALLS HAVE BEEN A PART OF CIVILIZATION since man figured out how to fell a tree and turn it into a protective structure. It's interesting to look at wood in this most simple of applications. But what will be shown in this chapter is something much more complicated: patina, texture, craftsmanship, warmth, artisanship — the beauty of natural woodwork and how it takes hold of the senses upon entering a room, captivating us with its warmth and delighting us with its three-dimensional beauty.

Wood paneling looks great with modern seating.

Grand paneling for a grand space.

Interest is created with molding.

Wood coupled with wallcoverings.

Design by Rebecca Shearn, Interiors by Decorating Den

Extremely modern and rich.

A very different look with horizontal plank positioning.

About wood

Wood as a decoration and enhancement to a room is a wonder to behold: consider patina, texture, craftsmanship, warmth, artisanship — all there in the beauty of natural woodwork and how it takes hold of the senses upon entering a room, captivating us with its warmth and delighting us with its three-dimensional beauty.

It is well known that one of the trademarks of any fine home, from Europe to the U.S., is the employment of superior architectural woodwork. From the 15th century on, one can trace the development of artisan-crafted wood paneling, set into interior frameworks, as they worked their way into our homes. Purposeful, wood paneling was a means to seal off drafts or to insulate a room from the sometimes frigid quality of a stone wall; but more so— wood was an exemplary vehicle for artistic expression through the intricate carving of motifs and repetitive patterns upon it.

Note that the Palace of Versailles has many fine examples of complex and elaborately carved paneling.

By the 18th century, the beauty of wood wall interiors incorporating wainscoting or boiserie was at its heyday. And yet, like all forms of custom craftwork, the scarcity of materials and the rising costs of woodworkers pushed the decorative wood wall into the homes of only the very wealthy.

But wood walls are also found in other applications: log homes of the American pioneers were incredibly beautiful in their natural state, carved to fit snugly, one log atop the next, interlocked. The first log cabins built in the U.S. were constructed in what is now southeast Pennsylvania in 1640; walls were either left natural or, later as log homes hit their stride, the interior walls were covered with lath and

Red tone wood paneling invites.

Inset panels frame artwork.

plaster, so that they could then be layered with wallpaper or paint.

Today, while the fees are still high for custom work, inventive technologies have afforded many homeowners the opportunity to enjoy the luxury of wood without prohibitive costs. Wainscoting can be picked up at your nearest home improvement center, interlocking together easily through tongue and groove. Beautiful moldings, chair rails, panels and more can enhance a dreary area, bringing warmth and beauty with natural good looks.

Of course, beauty doesn't always go without its cost. Though price will vary depending upon the type and grade of wood selected, whether it is carved or embellished or left to show its natural beauty, in general, an eight square foot wainscoting kit can cost around $80 and from there, on upwards into the hundreds and thousands of dollars depending upon many factors. One woodworking company estimat-

ed that a 12' x 12' room, excluding openings such as doors and windows, covered floor to ceiling in cherrywood panels, could cost upwards of $25,000 and take six to eight weeks to complete.

Note also that, as you probably could have guessed, the type of wood selected will make an impact on the emotions evoked in a room. For example, maple, a lighter more modern looking wood tone, will offer up a different response than a dark wood like ebony.

When decorating, think not just about the various kinds of paneling, but also doors, mantles, columns, cornices and moldings, too.

A few more things

If you are unable to cover your entire wall with wood paneling, consider how you can add wood into the mix in smaller dosages. From the floor up, you can add wood in the form of baseboards (where the

A great, inviting look for the home office.

floor and the wall meet horizontally and vertically); case moldings, a material used to trim a doorway, window or archway; a chair rail, which is a piece of molding that is installed about 24 to 48 inches from the floor but usually about 36 inches — which is approximately the height of most chair backs and casegoods; and wainscoting, also known as paneling, which was developed to cover a water wicking effect called "rising damp," a common problem in the early years of home construction.

Let's discuss paneling for a short moment. Traditional paneling is the style you may be most familiar with. With raised and inset areas resembling vertical rectangles, this is a classic early Colonial style. Formal and simple, it is a timeless, elegant panel.

Beadboard paneling, also a fixture in homes since the 19th century, is a more casual style of wall covering used in summer cottages, kitchens, bathrooms and porches. Characterized by a series of thin, raised vertical strips — or beads — that flow along each panel, it was originally assembled out of scraps of wood.

The vertical lines of the beadboard style add a sense of height to a room. And notice some of the latest furniture styles, especially from larger retailers such as Crate and Barrel or Pottery Barn: beadboard stylings have been incorporated into furniture designs as well.

Craftsman paneling is a combination of a recessed square stacked atop a recessed vertical rectangle. Usually, this paneling will extend up about three quarters of the wall height, though a range of heights is available. Also called "Classic American" paneling, it is often used in more highly trafficked areas, such as foyers, livingrooms, conference and dining rooms.

Classic Modern paneling takes the recessed rectangle and places it horizontally to create a smooth, elongated and minimalist appearance. If you are looking for a panel style that will complement the work of such luminaries as Frank Lloyd Wright, Alvar Aalto and Walter Gropius, to name a few, this is the paneling you should choose.

Also, don't forget to place a header on top of a doorway for added emphasis, or even consider a decorative window sill to increase the presence of wood in your home.

Ceiling molding echoes the walls below.

Luscious details in a room made for relaxation.

Vertical strips with oversized molding.

Wood complements the luxe fabrics.

Heavy wood paneling is imposing and beautiful.   Gorgeous two-tone coloration.

A stately home.

Combine wood paneling with built-in bookcases.

Checkerboard-style paneling.

Intricate wood detailing is completely elegant, a timeless look.

No other wall treatment could have been as perfect for this space.

Stately woodwork enhances floor, wall and ceiling.

Wood and wallpaper combine for an Art Deco look.

Varying inset sizes create big interest.

Gorgeous built-in wine rack.

Vertical paneling elongates the area.

(above) Quaint vertical wood strips. (below) Horizontal/vertical piecing create a sense of movement.

(above) Half install allows decor color change much more easily. (below) One third height with inset panels.

Smaller scale log walls.   Terrific vertical paneling.

Maple paneling in a natural finish looks very modern.

Insets make a great place for vertical art pieces.

Sleek paneled room divider/fireplace.

A sleek look, providing a clean, fresh line moving from room to room.

Fresh country looks.   A beautiful bathroom installation.

Clean white paneling offers inviting spaciousness.

White-washed tone-on-tone paneling for simple elegance.

Half-pillars make a statement in an entryway.

Very sleek and clean.   Varying panel sizes are visually interesting.

Intricate detailing delights.

Wood paneling makes a terrific room divider.

Built-in bookcases add to the value of the home.

Design by Lisa Landry, Interiors by Decorating Den

From floor to ceiling, wood delivers.

Painted wood is very appealing.

Traditional chair rail paneling.

Modern beauty.

(above) Who would have thought red toned paneling could be so rich and elegant?

Wood combined with marble and decorative painted inlays.

Don't forget that paneling can conform to angles!

Floor to ceiling beauty. Perfect in a formal sitting area.

(below) Magnificent paneling imparts regal air.

Ceilings

Hopelessly underutilized, the ceiling, our interior sky, is a wide swath of space typically painted white and left to harbor lighting fixtures and the occasional cobweb.

Look at the sky, if you will. It is a beautiful cap to Mother Nature, sometimes mottled blue, or thunderstorm green, streaked with pinks and purples at sunrise, a lipstick sunset at evening. So why do so many of us neglect the possibilities that our own ceilings present?

Decorating the fifth wall is attention to detail at its best, creating drama in the dining room or a calm, restful environment in the bedroom. The decorated ceiling pulls our eyes upward, creating a sense of satisfied completion to any interior.

A tiled kitchen ceiling — stunning and unique. Photo courtesy of Sarah Barnard Design

Accent lighting

Accent lighting

Fabric

Fabric

Fabric

Medallion

Medallion

Painted

Painted

Painted

Painted-decorative

Painted-decorative

Painted-decorative

Painted-decorative

Painted-decorative

Tin

Tin

Wallpaper-borders

Wallpaper-borders

Wallpaper

Wallpaper

Wallpaper

Wallpaper

Wallpaper

Wood-beams

Wood-beams

Wood-beams

Wood-beams

Wood-beams

Wood-beams

Wood-other

Wood-other

Wood-other

Wood-other

Wood-other

Wood-other

Intricate, painted scrolling makes use of the ceiling canvas.

(above) Centering the table under the inset is effective.
(right) A wood plank ceiling adds to the rustic flair.

About ceilings

Just about any kind of surface that can be applied to a wall can also be applied to a ceiling, with a couple of variations. For the most part, however, you can look at many of the surfacing products we have already covered to serve as your guide: paint, wallpaper, fabric, tile and stone, wood, metal and glass, as well as plastic and plaster.

Indeed, as I mentioned earlier, ceilings are hopelessly underutilized, so to see a ceiling decorated to its full potential, be it subtly colored a light sky blue or draped with a luxurious fabric, it is a joy and surprise to behold.

Consider adding a medallion around a hanging light fixture such as a chandelier, adding a line of substantial beams, a bit of iron scrollwork, a glass skylight, or using plaster to add texture and detail. Stencil stars, add a wallpaper border, add pressed tin tiles ... it's all up to you.

Why is it that tradition calls for a white ceiling? Neutrality is the most common answer — but that might not be the best for the room. Consider if you have a high ceiling and want to make it appear lower. Will white do the trick? Absolutely not. You should consider a brown, dark blue or charcoal tone to bring that ceiling down visually. If you want to raise the roof, consider a light yellow, blue or peach. Another consideration: finish. A gloss in the paint you select will amplify light, while a matte finish will absorb it.

Ceiling imperfections can be covered with fabric, wood beams or other materials.

Speaking of amplification: accoustical tiles, wood or fabric can help absorb extraneous noise.

A few more things

Are you inside your home right now? Okay — here's your assignment. Look up. What do you see? I'll bet it's white. Now go lie down in bed. Look at the ceiling. Doesn't it suddenly seem awfully plain? Especially in the bedroom, we are quite aware of our ceilings. Do you sometimes take a nap on the couch? Wouldn't it be nice to see something other than boring white when you open your eyes?

(above) Stained glass ceiling enchants. (below) Horizontal beams elongate the area.

(above) Plaster ceiling medallion. (below) Intricate wood strip patterning draws the eye up.

Beams extend to the wood walls in a classic living area.

White beamsalso hold lighting fixtures.

Undeniably clean and classic appearance.

Sleek wood ceiling shows shallower criss-cross pattern.

Dramatic checkerboard beams cap the room.

Eyes are drawn upward with columns that match ceiling beams.

Floral detailing on the ceiling matches the light fixture.

Sky blue ceiling enhances the height of the room.

A cloud motif offers a restful retreat.

Design by Wilma Schuiten, Interiors by Decorating Den

Unusual chandelier is enhanced with cloud detailing on the ceiling.

Design by Heidi Sowatsky, Interiors by Decorating Den

Blue ceiling ties the room together.

Mottled green ceiling echoes patterning in the wallpaper.

Art Deco detailing is crisp and unique in the bedroom.

Dramatic multi-colored ceiling inset.

Ceiling painted to resemble sky with wisps of clouds.

Elaborate plaster, wood trim and paint merge to dramatic result.

(above) Stunning bedroom made unique with beautiful ceiling. (below) Tin ceiling adds class.

(above) Gorgeous ceiling work makes for a memorable room. (below) Blues and beige add height.

(above) Glossy white paneled ceiling brightens the room, while adding detail.

Medallion for lighting enhances ceiling.

Elaborate ceiling medallion with detail picked up on molding.

A fancifully painted childs' bedroom.

High ceiling is accentuated with heavy wood beams.

Wallpaper moves from walls to ceiling in this formal bedroom.

Panels of red offset by the white beams tie the room together perfectly.

Wallpaper on the ceiling resembles an ornate tin application.   Coordinating wallpaper on the ceiling pulls the room together.

A bold ceiling medallion showcases sky and cloud decorative ceiling mural.

Wood paneling is a sleek solution.

Charcoal gray ceiling imparts sophisticated air.

Beams run between each of the arched access areas.

Shiny tin ceiling dazzles.

Dark paneled ceilings match cabinetry perfectly.

High ceiling is accentuated with heavy wood beams.

Bright and airy elevation in the kitchen dining area.

Elegant glass ceiling for a formal area.

Rich plum coloration on a metal ceiling.

Light wood ceiling is as eye-catching as the darker floor.

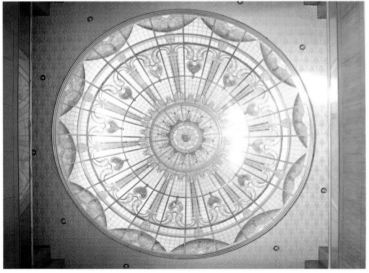

Beautiful stained glass ceiling.

Rich chocolate ceiling tones pop against lighter wood floor.

Design by the team of Barrett/Jakob/Zimmerman/Cochran, Interiors by Decorating Den

Tented fabric ceiling.

Mottled decoratively painted ceiling is beautifully warm.

Milk chocolate ceiling with seafoam green walls.

Undulating rows of fabric create an elegant ceiling.

Beautiful fabric treatment on the ceiling continues the luxurious feeling the furnishings and window treatments have imparted.

High solid tenting creates a gazebo feel indoors.

(above) Beautifully paneled ceiling draws the eye straight up.

Wood walls couple with strip ceiling to great effect.

Long planks on the ceiling add to the natural decor.

Sleek modern wood strip ceiling.

Long lengths of thin wood strip on the ceiling.

(below) Bright wood ceiling caps an awesome room.

Floor Coverings

HOW OFTEN DO YOU WALK INTO A ROOM ... AND look down? That's the sad truth about flooring — it is the unsung hero of many a room, bolstering the beauty of the walls and windows ... a quiet type, but one who takes more abuse than any other. Animal claws, cleats, high heels, furniture dragged across its sturdy beauty — our floors deserve much better than we ever give them time for. They must be vacuumed or swept? Such a bother! And yet without a beautiful floor, your room is incomplete.

So as you contemplate your next floor covering, buy the best you can afford. Be kind to it, and in return, it will provide you with years of unending beauty.

Gleaming wood floor is enhanced with vibrant rugs.

Hardwood: ash

Hardwood: bamboo

Hardwood: beech

Hardwood: brazilian cherry

Hardwood: cypress

Hardwood: engineered wood

Hardwood: heart cypress select

Hardwood: inlay/medallion accent

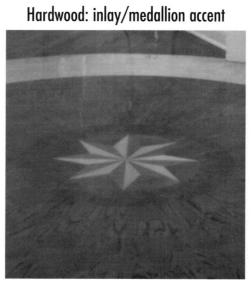

Hardwood: jarrah

Hardwood: karri

Hardwood: maple

Hardwood: parquet

Hardwood: oak

Hardwood: pegged plank

Hardwood: reclaimed/recycled

Hardwood: rose river gum

Hardwood: spotted gum

Hardwood: wood variety

Carpet & rugs: berber

Carpet & rugs: blend (silk & wool)

Carpet & rugs: broadloom

Carpet & rugs: frieze

Carpet & rugs: hand-knotted

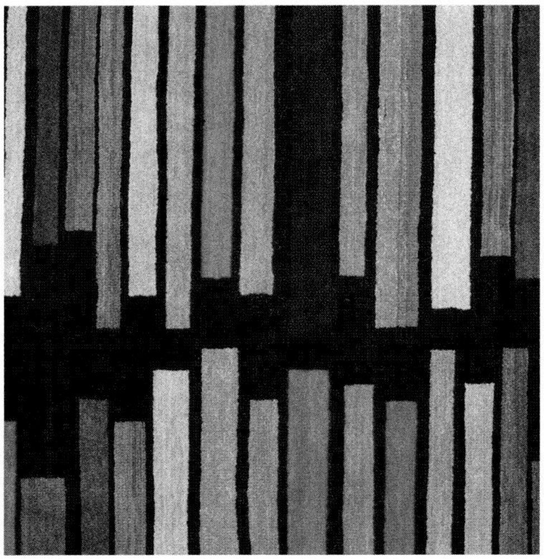

Carpet & rugs: hand-tufted

Carpet & rugs: lamontage

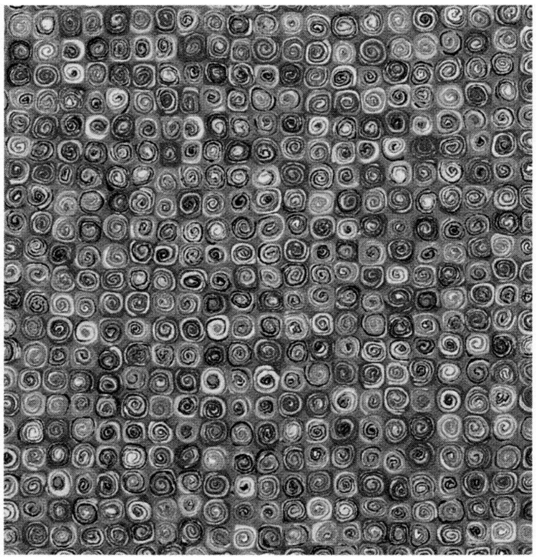

Carpet & rugs: nylon

Carpet & rugs: oriental

Carpet & rugs: patterned

Carpet & rugs: polypropylene

Carpet & rugs: recycled plastic

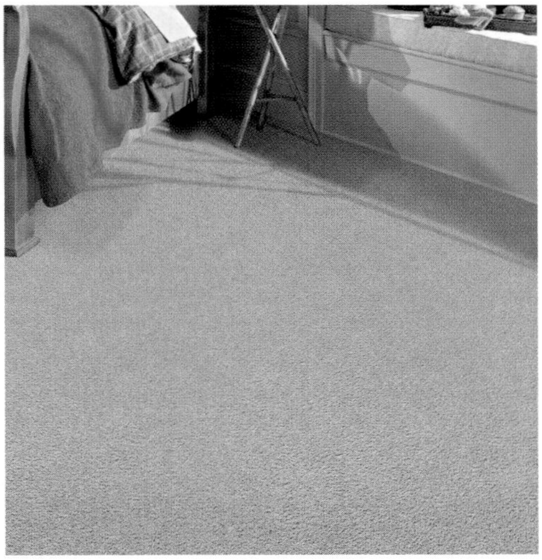

Carpet & rugs: sheepskin

Carpet & rugs: wool

Laminate: tile

Laminate: tile

Laminate: tile

Laminate: tile

Laminate: tile

Laminate: wood/beech

Laminate: wood/brazilian cherry

Laminate: wood/herringbone merbau

Laminate: wood/oak

Laminate: wood/red oak

Laminate: wood/walnut

Laminate: wood/western maple

Resilient: cork

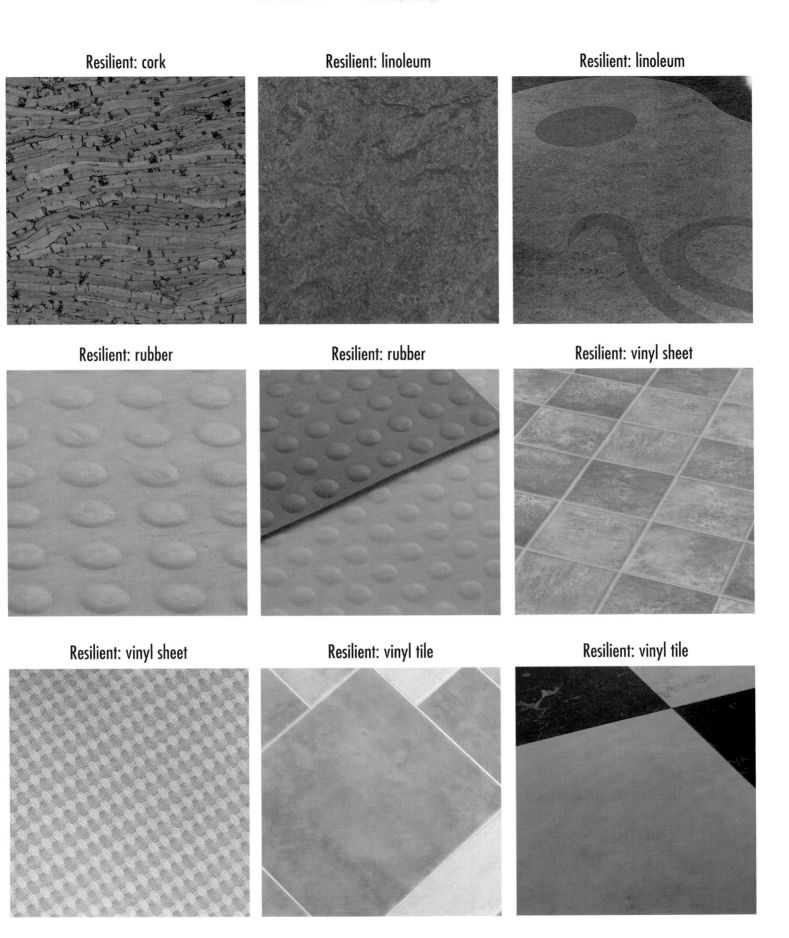

Resilient: cork

Resilient: linoleum

Resilient: linoleum

Resilient: rubber

Resilient: rubber

Resilient: vinyl sheet

Resilient: vinyl sheet

Resilient: vinyl tile

Resilient: vinyl tile

Tile & stone: basketweave pattern

Tile & stone: ceramic

Tile & stone: clay

Tile & stone: field tile

Tile & stone: glass

Tile & stone: glass

Tile & stone: glazed

Tile & stone: leather

Tile & stone: limestone

Tile & stone: marble

Tile & stone: metal

Tile & stone: mosaic

Tile & stone: porcelain

Tile & stone: porcelain

Tile & stone: quarry

Tile & stone: slate

Tile & stone: slate

Tile & stone: terrazzo

Hardwood

THE TIMELESS LOOK OF WOOD FLOORING CONNECTS us with nature and suggests a warmth and beauty which only increases in value as the years pass.

The resonant tone of heels on hardwood; the imperfections that a nail hole or a bird beak will imbue are comforting, especially to those who are aware that the gifts of our natural world are slowly dwindling. And because of this natural beauty, the very nature of the imperfection of wood makes it perfect to many.

Consider the popularity of recycled or reclaimed wood, the environmentally-friendly aspects of harvesting bamboo ... the complete permanence of a flooring material that can be abused over and over, then sanded, coated and restored to its original luster.

High gloss finish is so elegant.

Star medallion.

(above) Side set squares accent a hallway.

(below) Rich planks look terrific.

A variety of hardwood in this colorful medallion.

Premium select vertical grain heart pine.

Canadian birch solid alternating size strips.

About hardwood

There are four different types of wood flooring products available: reclaimed wood, solid wood, engineered wood and wood alternatives.

Within these groups, there are over 50 domestic and exotic species currently being used in flooring — a staggering amount of choices, especially when you factor in finish colors!

Let's examine the four categories of wood flooring products, to help you zero in on what might suit your next project best.

Let's first turn an eye to reclaimed wood.

Reclaimed wood is for the customer who is environmentally conscious, and has the money to back it up. Typically recycled from abandoned barns, railroad ties, old mill lumber lost at the bottom of a river and more, it is re-sanded, re-planed and otherwise honed to renewed beauty. And think about this: some reclaimed wood is no longer available as new flooring material — a big plus for any client who wants something nobody else has. These hard-to-acquire "cradle-to-cradle" woods include heart pine, redwood and chestnut.

Understand, though, that reclaimed wood flooring is often difficult to obtain in large quantities, due to the "scavenger"-type nature of acquisition. Be certain that when the product is ordered, you have enough resources to not only cover the floor, but also have back-up product should warping or cupping occur during installation.

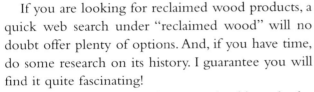

Classic pecan with grain variations and knots.   Pecan plank engineered wood flooring.

If you are looking for reclaimed wood products, a quick web search under "reclaimed wood" will no doubt offer plenty of options. And, if you have time, do some research on its history. I guarantee you will find it quite fascinating!

Moving on, solid wood, is very durable and relatively soft underfoot. Some of the more popular types of solid wood floors are pine, oak, teak and walnut. The cost of a solid product will vary depending upon the type and grade of wood selected, but will usually be less expensive than solid reclaimed wood.

Solid wood can be cut into planks of varying sizes, as well as used for intricate floor patterns such as medallions and parquet. Easy to refinish, distinctive due to natural patterns and markings and exceptionally strong, solid wood is a terrific choice for many areas of the home.

Best, it can be sanded and refinished for generations, making it an optimal choice for those of you who want something permanent.

Finally, remember that wood can be negatively affected by moisture and fluctuations in humidity, so its not suited for high-moisture or below-grade (such as a basement) areas.

Engineered wood is a type of flooring created with a layered construction. This reduces the twisting and cupping that may occur in solid wood planks and strips. In some ways, it is similar to laminate flooring, which we will discuss shortly, in that there is a top

Reclaimed white oak, precision milled.

Canadian maple plank, 3.25" wide.

Creating the illusion of extended length with alternating strips.

"beauty" layer that may conceal a less favorable wood product beneath.

This type of flooring is less expensive than both reclaimed and solid wood floors and also handles changes in temperature and humidity better than solid wood.

What is terrific about engineered flooring is that it makes exotic woods more available, as some just can't be produced in solid styles. Better yet, engineered wood can be installed on any level of the home, as it handles expansion and contraction with increased ease.

It is good to note that engineered wood is not a product that performs as well in high traffic areas. When engineered wood is assembled, each layer is set at a 90-degree angle from the previous layer, for strength. Grain mismatch may appear if the top layer is often refinished and/or sanded.

Finally, bamboo flooring is grouped into the hardwood category, but is actually (as you may know) grass, with a wood-like stem. Environmentalists agree that this product is highly sustainable. Bamboo is taken from the original rough, round cane and cut into smooth, beautiful planks.

Don't be concerned about the possibility of hungry koala bears losing their favorite treat: the type of bamboo used for flooring is the Moso species; it is not the type used for animal food!

Remarkably, despite being a grass, bamboo is as solid as maple and more stable than red oak, so you can expect a superior product with outstanding durability.

Whether left in its natural tone of light blonde or stained to a variety of colors, bamboo is an environmentally friendly option for the "green" consumer.

Pacific bamboo flooring, durable and innovative.

Unique light color and fine grain shine in maple.

A few more things

So, with all of the wonderful things I have outlined about wood floors, you might think that there isn't a reason in the world why you shouldn't choose it. Actually, there are a few reasons, but for the most part, drawbacks will include issues related to moisture (don't use wood in a bathroom, for example, unless you make generous use of bath mats and rugs); and cost. I can guarantee that if you want a beautiful solid wood floor, you will pay for it with a grand sum. It's important to remember that this truly is the kind of floor that will last a lifetime when cared for properly.

One other drawback to consider — and this is in regard to refinishing a well-loved floor. It isn't quick to refinish — and it's also stinky. A typical turn-around time is about three days for the work involved with a couple extra days added in for alleviation of the scent related to the type of finish you select. To break it down, one day is needed to sand the floor and remove all related dust generated, one day to apply the first coat of finish, one day to apply the second coat...and then overall dry time. Plus if you have animals, you should consider boarding them because there should be no stepping on the floor until it is absolutely and completely dry. And, you will need to remove all furniture from the area being refinished. The best thing you can do is to take a vacation, have the floors done and when you return, you will have a wonderful new floor awaiting you. Believe me, it's worth every penny.

Time worn hand scraped in concert with modern amenities.

Tight grained Brazilian cherry.　　Detailed compass floor medallion.

Multi tones catch the eye.

Four wood inlay: cherry, poplar, wenge and oak.

Hand-scraped vintage walnut planks.

(above) The coffee colored floor boards ground this sophisticated room.

Premium three-strip teak flooring.

Karri wood offers pale pink to reddish brown overtones.

 Multi-tone wood floor.  Black walnut floor is striking.

(below) Premium plank ash has beveled edges and ends.

English walnut strip engineered flooring.

Hand-scraped so no two boards are alike.

Wide planks and a high gloss finish sparkle.

Thin strip flooring mirrors wallpaper stripe size.

Two inch strips, highly polished, appear rich and luxurious.

Five types of machine cut wood create this floor.

Wide planks emphasize details of grain patterns and textures.

Five types of machine cut wood create this floor.

Antique distressed oak retrieved from old buildings.

Elaborate machine cut wood medallion.

Wide, sophisticated plank flooring.

(above) All eyes are on the floor when multi-colored wood is in use.

Rich, warm flooring tone makes cream furnishings pop.

A lifetime of beauty with natural hardwood floors.

(above) Engineered wood flooring in a spice oak coloration.

Caramelized vertical grain bamboo flooring. Photo by Steven Young and courtesy of Teragren LLC.

Carpet & Rugs

NOTHING FEELS BETTER UNDERFOOT THAN LUXURI-

OUS CARPET, an unending array of little fibers nestled

together to capture warmth and offer cush, bolstered by

a good padding to prolong its life and provide added

insulation from noise.

Carpeting is true luxury for your feet, and the array

of styles and colors offered for both carpet and rugs is

truly staggering. From hard-wearing stain resistant floor

coverings, best for use in high traffic areas (consider the

sturdy berber) to the type of carpet only meant for bare

feet in front of a fireplace (think sheepskin) to the

environmentally-friendly (but there's no way you'd be

able to tell) carpet made from recycled plastic drink

bottles, there is a soft bit of flooring just waiting to be

your next underfoot dream.

Soft colors are welcoming in a relaxed
kitchen dining area.

Soft and resilient.

(above) Terrific texturing and style.

(below) Fun patterning on the floor.

Walking steps has never been more satisfying!

Cool blues and greens enliven the beige background.

A great, comfortable space for work or play.

About carpet & rugs

As you probably know, some types of carpet and rugs are more durable than others due to the combination of pile fiber, fiber weight and pile density.

What's pile, you ask? Well, pile is the term that refers to the visible surface of the carpeting. It's also sometimes called "face" or "nap."

Carpet and rugs, for which the color combinations, patterns and styles are many, are wonderful for camouflaging a well-worn floor, for sound and shock absorption and also offer maximum insulation for those times when bare feet need warmth.

Remember, though, that any kind of fabric flooring will be a disastrous choice in areas of high moisture. Plus, improper dying can cause color transfer, backing can separate from the fiber and more. Finally, lack of maintenance and dirt build up will abrade the fibers, crushing and matting them, and cause staining too.

A few of the more popular textures include:

> Cut & loop, a mix of both straight and looped fibers which provide surface texture

> Shag, in which loops are cut to create nice "cush" underfoot (also known as cut pile)

> Frieze (*free-zay*), a tightly curled cut pile that masks vacuum cleaner marks and footprints

> Level loop, level uncut loops of the same height and size; very suitable for high traffic areas

> Multi-level loop, which offers two to three loop heights to create patterning

Two color patterning is warm and wonderful.

Playful plaid makes for an inviting space.

> Plush, a velvety cut pile that offers a smooth surface, but will show every imprint; and finally,

> Saxony, a cut pile with an extra twist in the yarn to create a dense, sophisticated look

One more thing: it's important to know that there are two categories of carpet fiber: natural and man-made. Natural fibers include wool, silk, coir, jute, sisal and flax. Man-made types include nylon, polyester, acrylic, etc.

The reason I bring this up is because you need to know that in general, man-made fibers excel at maintaining color, resisting soil, stains and wear. Some of the natural fibers, especially wool, come close, but not quite enough.

Note that some carpet is recyclable — the problem is that only about four percent of waste carpet gets proper end-use handling.

If you are interested in "green" carpet, there is plenty to choose from. Most "green" carpeting is made from 100% post-consumer recycled food and drink containers. By purchasing one square yard of recycled carpeting, for example, you will be keeping approximately 40 plastic containers out of our landfills.

As for rugs, their most compelling aspect is that they can be picked up and moved with little effort, so rugs of all kinds are perfect for those who lease their homes — or those who like to change out their décor frequently. Cleaning is also a breeze, as a rug

This broadloom, the new "shag," is a high-twist soft frieze.

Ivory sheepskin, 60 millimeters deep.   A simple, natural rug ties this modern room together.

can be rolled up and transported easily.

There are many rugs styles available, but some of the most popular include:

> Aubusson, a tapestry-style rug featuring floral and architectural motifs
> Braided, a casual, circular rug which is usually reversible
> Brocade, an embossed or engraved rug using heavily twisted yarn
> Dhurrie, a thin, flatwoven rug constructed of cotton or wool
> Flokati, an elegant hand-woven wool rug, soft to the touch, originating in Greece
> Fur, such as alpaca or sheepskin, which is sheared from the animal and then woven onto a backing; or hide (such as cowhide or bear skin)
> Gabbeh, a coarse rug recognized more for its artistic value than its comfort
> Kilim, a reversible flatwoven rug with a smooth surface
> Mahal, a medium weave rug with a soft hand, beautiful design and soft color combination
> Needlepoint, a hand-made rug that is created using a pattern-stenciled canvas
> Oriental, a rug native to the Middle or Far East that is known for its many patterns and colorations
> Persian, a rich, beautiful wool or silk rug with graceful floral designs and delicate colorations
> Rag, a casual hand-tied rug made from colorful cotton scraps, often seen in kitchens
> Savonnerie, a hand-knotted rug typically made in pastel tones with floral medallions; and finally
> Tibetan, a hand-knotted wool rug made with a special technique of knotting.

Like carpet, a rug is affected by the type of material used in its construction. Also, consider that many people want a rug not just for its insulating properties but also because many rugs can be considered works of art.

I suppose you might wonder what determines the price of a rug. After all, you can find rugs for as little as $4.99 at your local wholesaler, to upwards of five digits — and quite honestly, some may appear to be identical at first glance!

The factors that determine a rug price include beauty, craftsmanship, age, condition, rarity and

Leaf carpet pattern is subtle but also works so well in blending other fabric elements in the room.

Playful teal brightens a rec room. Rosy pink and beige form for a soft interior.

demand. Remember that some handmade rugs are akin to furniture in that there are degrees of quality and beauty to be upheld. Manufactured rugs will inevitably be less expensive because the cost to produce them is so much lower.

Know that weaving and dye techniques will factor into the cost, too.

Above all else, buy the best-crafted carpet you can afford. You will be rewarded with years of great looks and performance.

A few more things

Let's just talk about two parts to the carpet that you don't really see, but will make a world of difference in performance: the backing and the padding.

The backing holds the carpet fibers in place; it's an anchor — in the same way, you might reason, that soil is the anchor for grass. With tufted carpet, there are two parts to the backing: the primary back, which the yarn is inserted into and the secondary backing, which is a layer laminated or bonded onto the primary back to make the piece more stable, yet still semi-pliable. These kinds of backing can hail

from a variety of materials, both natural and synthetic: jute, polyurethane and nylon, to name a few.

With woven carpet, the backing is more like the "back" side of, well, something that has been woven, with warp and weft threads. Many of the rugs you see will be of the woven variety.

But beyond what it's made from, backing also provides support and insulation and helps resist mold, mildew and rot.

Backing is not to be confused with padding, which is an additional layer placed directly on the floor. Certainly, you do not have to put a pad underneath carpeting, but I highly suggest you *do*. Padding will prolong the life of the carpet and add more cush underneath. It will also provide additional insulation and another barrier against anything mold or mildew related.

Unfortunately, because this is an important layer of defense against undesirable elements, padding is treated with a variety of substances to help in the battle. These substances, usually chemical, can cause "off-gassing," an evaporation of the chemicals. Depending upon the person and the product, this

(above) Bold patterning, rich red and terracotta tones are eye-catching. (below) Great flirty patterning and color.

Green-tinted carpet brings the outdoors in.

negative change in air quality can be quite intolerable. It is often suggested that a product is allowed to "breathe" prior to installation, or that a person waits a few days before living in the environment.

You might be surprised to find that off-gassing can occur for years afterward, but the levels are so low, they are indistinguishable, except to the most sensitive of noses. If you have any concerns about off-gassing, it is best to address them prior to the purchase of a pad.

The good news is that there have been some developments, such as the "frothed foam" pad, that has virtually undetectable volatile organic compounds (VOCs). Extremely thick, it will resist indenting from the weight of furniture and is made without petroleum products. Sunflower oil is used in its construction instead. It also is not supposed to crumble or break down over time.

Carpet pads fall into a couple of categories: Foam, Rubber and Fiber. Each have different insulating properties and some are better suited for commercial and high-traffic areas than others. A word of warning: padding is not cheap. It will definitely add a worthy amount to the price of your carpet. A rule of thumb is that a pad may cost about $1.50 per square foot, which, if you are looking at an average basement size of 300 square feet, it means you will have another $450 added onto the cost of your product.

It follows then that you may be tempted into buying a carpeting system that includes a free pad with purchase. This is not always a good thing. Some manufacturer's warranties will be void if you do not use its specified pad and also, it may not be the best kind of support and protection for the type of traffic you anticipate or the environment it will be installed into.

One more thing: do't go overboard with a pad purchase and buy more than you need. Consider radiant heat, for example. If you buy too thick a pad, will the heat be able to work its way up through that thick pad, through the backing and fibers and finally to your toes? Perhaps not as effectively. Consider all options and needs before you take that plunge.

Rough, nubby rug contrasts with the moss green velvet sofa, harmoniously.

Nubby jute rug is welcoming in the sun porch.   Salmon-toned textured broadloom carpet.

The color of wealth and luxury, luxurious underfoot.   The braided rug — a classic covering for the floor.

Blue and red create warm tones underfoot.

Treads and risers, covered in style.

Muted but strong colors tie the color scheme together.

The padded path to true decadence.

Rich tones tie the room together stylishly.

The right tones in a rug will also enhance the wood below.

So cute, you'll want to play indoor hopscotch!

A rich, elegant color palette.

Low pile cushions the foot but doesn't obstruct chairs.

Hard-wearing Berber boasts a larger yarn.

Rug tones pick up all of the colors inside — and outside.

Dark border draws the circling furniture together.

This rug grounds the whole area, exuding feminine spirit.

A strong, beautiful floor covering for high traffic areas.

Deep pile rug makes hard floors soft.

Rug protects the floor from daily in and out chair scraping.

(above) Earthy pastels delight. Design by Lois Pade, Interiors by Decorating Den

Andy Warhol©The Andy Warhol Foundation

Neutral tones create drama.

Geometrics are still very popular patterns.

An underfoot focal point.　Black and tan — a stylish combination.

(below) Animal prints are still trendy. Design by Cathy Osika, Interiors by Decorating Den

Laminate

YOU HAVE REACHED THE CHAPTER COVERING THE hottest floor covering developed in the past 30 years. Easy to install, resistant to dents, stains, cigarette burns and also known as "the great pretender" due to its chameleon-like ability to replicate many other kinds of more expensive flooring, laminate is perfect for high traffic areas. Sales of laminate flooring hit the billion dollar-plus mark for the first time about five years ago, showing a 32.5 percent growth rate alone. Eighty percent of those sales went toward replacing an existing floor!

Why is it so popular? Well read on for more information on this versatile product.

Golden strip pecan laminate complements a checkerboard backsplash.

An unusual color combination is eye-catching.

Staggered color patterns.

Laminate installed with glue-free technology.

Sound inhibitor with moisture resistant feature in birch replica.

Extra durable, this is a very thick laminate.

Elm laminate is a full plank design with realistic knot holes.

About laminate

If you look at some of the laminate products installed today (and you will often see them used in commercial applications — a testament to durability), you will note that the beauty layer is so realistic, it may be difficult to determine that the flooring is, indeed, laminate.

Installed as a "floating" floor, in essence, installed directly over any other surface in a "click" joint tongue-and-groove assembly, laminate is very durable and resistant to stain. Better still, should problems occur, replacement of product is relatively easy. It also works very well below-grade, such as in a basement. And when I say floating floor, I mean it truly does "float." It is not attached to the subfloor underneath. No glue, nails or staples are needed, which is great for that basement I just mentioned, where you no doubt have a cement subfloor.

Another plus is that it is easy to transport. Think about the long, eight-foot or more planks of solid wood, for example — can you imagine the weight and cumbersome nature of the packaging? Laminate, on the other hand, is much thinner and is typically manufactured in four-foot lengths. Boxed up and lightweight, no doubt it's much easier to ship.

Drawbacks include the "sound" it creates. While it may look like a wood floor, for example, it may not necessarily *sound* like a wood floor when being trod upon. It can't be refinished or sanded and unfortunately, cheaper laminate products will show obvious

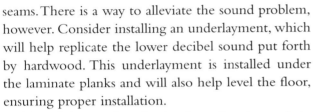
Classically elegant!   A subtle combination of three plank lengths.

seams. There is a way to alleviate the sound problem, however. Consider installing an underlayment, which will help replicate the lower decibel sound put forth by hardwood. This underlayment is installed under the laminate planks and will also help level the floor, ensuring proper installation.

You might wonder what laminate flooring truly is. I mentioned how realistic the flooring looks: it's pretty amazing how much the floor will look like wood or tile or stone, to name a few. So, does that mean that there is actually wood or stone in the flooring? Absolutely not. Let's examine laminate construction.

Laminate consists of four layers. Starting from the top and working down, the product consists of:
> a wear layer (the protective finish)
> a decorative layer (the "photograph" of the product it is mimicking)
> a fiberboard core (which provides impact protection and stability underfoot); and finally,
> a back layer, which helps with moisture resistance.

Each layer is important, but it is the decorative layer that most people find fascinating. Why? Because just as you could take a photograph and place it under a piece of glass — a manufacturer can do the same with laminate. While you may still associate laminate with the look of wood, you will see in ensuing photographs that tile replicas have become very popular.

Olive laminate in a three strip design.

Realistic textures are coupled with a moisture-resistant finish.

Laminate rendition of classic oak flooring.

New developments include wood/laminate hybrids, in which a wood veneer is used in place of the typical beauty layer, for the most realistic texturing available.

A few more things

You should note that lamimate planks typically need a "curing" time of about 48 hours to acclimate to the space they will be installed into. This is mostly about humidity levels. You want the boards to adapt before they are set, rather than after, of course.

Additionally, ask for products that use EIR

(embossed-in-register) texturing for the most realistic appearance. Add to that the new beveled edge look which mimics the edge of a solid wood product.

We have discussed some of the many advantages to installing a laminate floor. Here are a couple of other thoughts. For one, what do you know about tile floor installation? And I do mean that actual heavy and cumbersome tile. Well, if you have any experience or knowledge, one of the first things that may come to mind is the grout. If the grout has not been sealed properly, cleaning grout can become a

Natural varnished maple laminate.

Thin strip laminate — perfect for the kitchen.

major chore. Now, think about laminate flooring with a tile beauty layer. No more scrubbing. All you will need to do to clean your laminate floor is sweep to eliminate dust and dirt, use a manufacturer's recommended cleaner for spot cleaning or even just a simple solution of one part vinegar to two parts water — and that's it.

Another advantage is the very quick means of installation. After the two day curing time, go ahead and install the floor, clicking each piece together, one after the other. Most well-known brands will have mechanical loking systems that allow planks to be

precisely aligned and joined without using glue or special tools. You will find that the installation is one of the easiest around. Once you're done — go ahead and walk all over, drag your furniture back into place, hold a dance, even. And while I don't suggest that you leave a water spill down for any length of time, know that top manufacturers will seal the edges of their laminate products with wax, so that if a spill does happen, the seam between one piece and the next is not compromised.

Tying the room decor together elegantly.

Golden toned laminate in various combinations.

Butterscotch toned laminate.

Warm, subtle wood tones in laminate.

Dark varnished cherry laminate.

A replica of South Pacific Merbau wood.

Laminate does adapt well to stair treads.

Stunning color changes in a warm, winning surface.

(above) The look of tile — in laminate! (below) The look of tile — no messy grout to contend with!

(above) Laminate tile looks elegant. (below) Incredibly beautiful and so much easier to install than regular tile!

(above) In your most formal setting, consider the beauty and durability of laminate.

Travertine-style commercial grade laminate.

Registered embossing captures the texture of real tile.

Earth-toned laminate tile in a sunny getaway.

Emerald slate laminate in 16" x 16" tiles.

(below) High traffic areas are a great candidate for laminate flooring, due to its extreme durability.

Resilient

RESILIENT FLOORING IS NAMED AFTER ITS TYPE OF PERFORMANCE: hard-working, pliant and enduring. Offering a slight "give" when walked upon, resilients create a yielding and comfortable feel underfoot. This is a wide category of products including vinyl, linoleum, cork and rubber and is most often found in areas where flooring is ... shall we say ... well loved (kitchen, bathroom, mudroom, playrooms).

Of the four types, vinyl wins hands down in popularity due to its ease of installation and lower price point, but linoleum, for instance, is making headway due to resurging interest in retro design, as well as its "cradle-to-cradle" natural ingredients. Cork, another resilient experiencing a renaissance, is receiving accolades for its environmentally-friendly sustainable harvesting practices.

Linoleum makes color experimentation a wild success.

Cool tile for a hot room.

(above) Funky corks looks.
(below) Retro resilient rules!

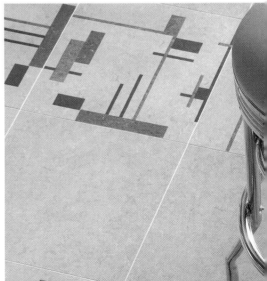

Wood tone in resilient flooring evokes warmth.

A tile look in vinyl sheet — so easy to install.

Funky vinyl sheet floors gleam with modern intensity.

About resilient flooring

Let's take a closer look at the four types of flooring that make up the resilient category:

Vinyl tile and sheet flooring is durable, stain and water resistant and comfortable underfoot. The colors and patterns available are very extensive, ranging from stone and wood looks to natural earth elements such as water and rocks.

It is available in two different wear layers: Urethane (a mid- to upper-end finish that protects the printed layer from most scuffs, spills and potential staining) and Poly-vinyl Chloride (PVC, a more basic wear layer that wile protective, does not safeguard the printed layer as effectively).

Advantages, in addition to those mentioned above, include ease of replacement when damaged, low maintenance and ability to adapt to uneven areas. Disadvantages include off-gassing in low-end varieties and worse, the product cannot be recycled.

To note its history, vinyl composition tile was first exhibited in 1933 in Chicago, but it wasn't marketed much until after the war years. However, by the 1970s, vinyl was the most popular flooring choice. Take a look at the Congoleum Company, which has been in business for over 120 years, if you'd like to track the development of this product.

The next category of resilient flooring is Cork, which has been around since its introduction in 1904, though it has only re-entered the public consciousness recently, due to its sustainable, environmentally-

Faithfully mimicking the appearance of real stone.

Wood plank design in a vinyl sheet flooring.

Stripes of earth toned linoleum warm up a kitchen.

friendly and durable qualities.

Stripped from the exterior of the cork oak tree (a sustainable practice that occurs about every nine years, leaving the tree intact and capable of bark regrowth), this renewable resource offers a pliable "give" underfoot due to its natural cellular structure. This renewable resource is available in four different types of readiness: unfinished, stained and ready to urethane; unfinished, unstained and ready to urethane; pre-finished and urethane covered; and pre-finished and vinyl-covered.

Sound absorbent, resistant to mold and mildew and fire-resistant, cork is available in tiles and planks, as well as finished and unfinished. It coloration is within the "natural" tone realm: brown, black and yellows, though it can be dyed other more intense colors as well.

Unfortunately, cork may initially emit a sort-of "earthy" odor and will also expand and contract slightly due to changes in humidity and temperature. If exposed to sun, the color will fade over time. Being it is a natural product, cork may succumb to abrasion with repeated foot traffic, though you will often see cork products in commercial areas such as museums, libraries and government centers.

Moving onto our next category, Rubber, you might think this kind of flooring is destined only for car dealerships, gymnasiums and cruise line decks. You might be surprised to discover that rubber flooring

Vinyl sheet mimics weathered slate.

Vinyl tile offers a 3-d effect, even though it has a smooth finish.

has been a part of the public eye since 1894! Patented by a Philadelphia architect, Frank Furness, the first rubber tile flooring was easy to clean and install, but unfortunately stained easily and deteriorated readily. It has come a long way since that time, believe me.

The good news is rubber is experiencing a Renaissance in revival due to its clear, uniform colors, dense, smooth surface and recyclability. While ultimately suited for extra heavy traffic and thus is used primarily in commercial areas, it is now found in residential exercise rooms, bathrooms — even laundry rooms. Its cost is somewhat high, but the hard-wearing qualities offset the initial expense, offering decades worth of usage.

What is rubber flooring anyway? Well, just what you may have suspected. Most rubber flooring is a combination of recycled automotive tires, post

industrial waste rubber and virgin rubber. It's good to know that the piles of discarded tires we have seen in the past are finally being put to good use.

Note, too, that while there is a lot of dark rubber flooring on the market, new innovation is allowing for some experimentation with vibrant colorations.

Finally, let's examine the gloriously colorful Linoleum, one of the oldest "earth-friendly" flooring materials around. Derived from a combination of linseed oil, cork and wood flour, pigments and pine resins, linoleum has benefited from improved technology to allow better and brighter color consistency.

Linoleum has had an interesting history, first surfacing in the late 1900s as an affordable flooring option. Being wood and tile was only affordable by the very wealthy, linoleum bridged that gap.

Unfortunately, it gained a bit of a reputation in

Vinyl sheet offers a naturally weathered stone tile look.

Electric blue is perfect for a sleek bathroom area.

the early to mid-20th century: You may recall the wild color and pattern experimentation of that time, when boomerang patterns, speckles and whimsical patterns decorated our ancestor's floors. Linoleum took on a kind of, well…tacky cachet. People began to turn their noses up at the product and sales plummeted.

Today, due to its biodegradable, recyclable properties (the word linoleum is Latin for flax (linum) and oil (oleum)) and its vibrant colors, as well as the allowing designers to use great imagination with color patterning and combinations, cutting and piecing at will, linoleum is again being shown in high-end interiors.

Though somewhat more labor intensive to install, it is well worth the end result: linoleum is easy on the feet, dust repellant due to its natural anti-static properties and is a snap to clean.

A few more things

While the choices for resilient flooring are still very firmly seeded in these four categories, technological advances have done away with most of the negatives and made these products a worthwhile investment. Second only to carpet in floor covering sales, the number of colors and patterns, the outstanding creativity waiting to be employed in your next decorating plan and the comfortable "foot-friendly" aspect to this flooring make it a wonderful choice.

Finally, an added binus is that resilient flooring in general requires little maintenance — mostly just a damp mop and a regular sweep.

High gloss looks.　Wide tile look makes the area appear larger.

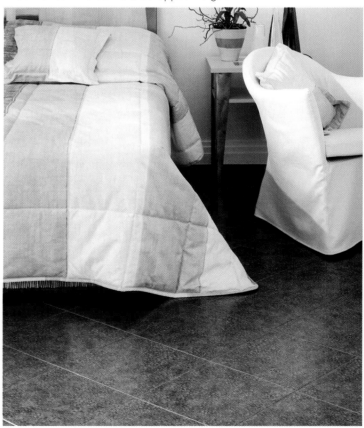

Stark black and white tile offers retro good looks.　Sleek bedroom floor shows a different twist on resilient flooring.

Light and medium colored cork. | Checkerboard pattern shows off varying cork tone beauty.

Beautiful and environmentally-friendly cork. | Comfortable cushion underfoot in a heavy use area.

Linoleum inlays create realistic rug and detail patterns.

Deep mottled red linoleum is seriously dramatic.

Wide swaths of red and brown cork create vibrancy.

(above) Peach, beige and green linoleum in a retro pattern.

Silver linoleum creates a high tech office backdrop.

Soothing pastel linoleum squares.

Muted taupe and beige linoleum — cool and modern.

Lilac-hued linoleum stripes pop against its darker counterpart.

(below) Dramatic linoleum detailing holds its own next to luxe casegoods.

Tile & Stone

THE APPEAL OF TILE AND STONE FLOORING HAS
spanned centuries, celebrating color and pattern
unmatched by any other flooring category. Glazed or
unglazed, extruded or pressed, slab, field, tumbled,
clefted, flamed, mosaic, glass, ceramic, porcelain ... the
list continues on and on. Tile and stone is visually rich,
transforming everything it touches with its infinite
color palette.

Today, the possibilities to blanket the floor with
luxurious stone and tile products are truly endless.
And even better, you may be indeed buying a bit of
history, perhaps millions of years old, even.

Rich warm tile tones make for a stunning home office.

Natural honed limestone.

Corner cutouts accent beautifully.

Glazed porcelain tile looks like slate.

Tile floor pattern mimics the ceiling above. Sleek!

Rustic tile, offset with decorative insets.

About tile & stone flooring

If you recall from the previous chapter on tile and stone for walls, there are plentiful products available today. One thing I did not discuss, however, is finish.

So, let's talk about it for a moment, shall we? The type of finish you select for your floor is mostly about safety and durability, because the floor is the one surface in your home that will take more abuse than any other. The way a piece of tile or stone is finished not only affects the way it looks, but also how it will perform.

A honed surface is machine-smoothed, stopping short of the polishing process. It will show fewer scratches than a polished surface and also allows for some wetness to be introduced to an area without worrying about slippage.

Have you heard of a polished surface? No doubt. What does that entail? Well, consider the diamond, the ultimate polished stone. Polishing natural stone

tile, while not as complicated as the diamond polishing process, has the same sort of result: that the natural stone crystals are polished to a beautiful glossy sheen, often so well that they are mirrorlike.

Here are three more finishes to consider.

A flamed surface is more textured and varied, created by "flaming" the top surface (yes, with fire), then rapidly cooling it. When the hot and cold are introduced one after the other, the surface of the stone will chip and raise, but not so that it is terribly rough. A flamed surface is good for areas where slip resistance is a concern, such as in bathrooms. Know that the color of the stone can change through flaming, much in the same way that many semi-precious and precious gemstones are heated to bring out their beautiful colorations.

A split faced stone tile is a roughly textured, but not as abrasive as flamed. Achieved by hand cutting and chiseling at the quarry, this technique exposes

Bluestone glazed porcelain floor tile with contour edging.

Rustic beauty with an elegant touch.

the natural cleft of the stone.

Finally, tumbled. Typically seen in marble and limestone, these machine-tumbled tiles exhibit a smooth or slightly pitted surface, and broken, rounded edges and corners.

As for surface decoration, tile can be:

> unglazed, which means that the range of color is limited by the actual color of the material is has been created from. This could be a light sandy tone to a red brick. Don't think for a minute that this isn't a handsome looking piece of tile, however. The natural beauty can be quite appealing in the proper installation.

> plain glazeed, which is a thin clear glaze applied to enhance the natural tone and also provide a bit of protection for the surface.

> Encaustic or inlaid decoration is a method in which a tile has been stamped with a decoration, and then that decoration is filled in with

white clay before it is glazed or fired. The two sections fuse together when they are fired.

> Hand-painted is a truly artistic effort, in which the surface of the tile is freely decorated in whatever colors and patterns the artist desires. Of course, these tiles will be quite expensive due to the amount of handwork and time employed. The piece is fired and the color becomes part of the tile.

> A carved tile is a relief carved into or a pattern pressed into the tile through the use of a wood block or other implement. This piece is usually painted as well to show contrast.

A few more things

What about mosaic and terrazzo floors? With mosaic, an artist will take small pieces of tile, sometimes even break ceramic pieces such as tea cups and saucers into manageable pieces, and assemble them

Polished porcelain tile with dainty detailing.   Matte glazed porcelain with scroll bordering.

in a way to create a pattern or picture. Then the entire creation is grouted and sealed.

One area that lends itself very well to mosaic is the shower stall. In a shower stall, there needs to be a slight pitch or angle toward the drain hole. This is hard to do with larger pieces of tile, but a snap with smaller pieces, as the diminuative size offers greater flexibility. Think about using one inch by one inch tile squares in a shower area for a positive outcome.

Terrazzo is a mixture of Portland Cement and marble, mixed together two parts marble to one part cement. After the mixture has been poured, it is sprinkled again with more marble and then dried. After drying, the floor is polished to a smooth finish and then given an application of protective sealer.

Finally, I'd like to talk about how hard a piece of tile is. Just as gemstones have different hardness values, so do tiles. These hardness values fall into five different groups, based primarily on foot traffic.

If you were to look at information on a particular tile, it will tell you what it is made of, the colors and styles available and you will also see something called "Durability Classification." That's the hardness.

Group I is a tile best suited for light traffic such as where bare or slippered feet are typical.

Group 2 is suited for medium traffic areas, usually further away from an entrance area.

Group 3 is for any home interior. This tile can handle just about any kind of foot traffic, including heavily traveled areas.

Group 4 is for heavily used entryways and light/medium commercial business areas.

Finally, Group 5 is the hardest tile, capable of withstanding extra heavy foot traffic.

Here's something to think about: For a wall application, any of these are hardness values are fine, but keep in mind that you might be buying or specifying more than you need. Walls don't need that kind of strength because they don't take the abuse that floors do. One other thing about hardness. The "harder" the tile, the more difficult it is to work with. It's harder to cut. It's harder to install, too — mostly because tile with a higher absorption rate will also grab the adhesive needed to install it. A piece of tile with a lower absorption rate will, in effect, repel the adhesive. So, note that if you are paying to have tile installed, your tile professional may charge more for his or her work.

A variety of colors form a fascinating pattern.

Polished basketweave pattern in marble.

Randomly cut stones are fit together stylishly.

Floor and backsplash harmonize to great result.

(above) Glazed porcelain floor tile in a classic pattern. (below) Natural stone tile is capable of handling wet floors easily.

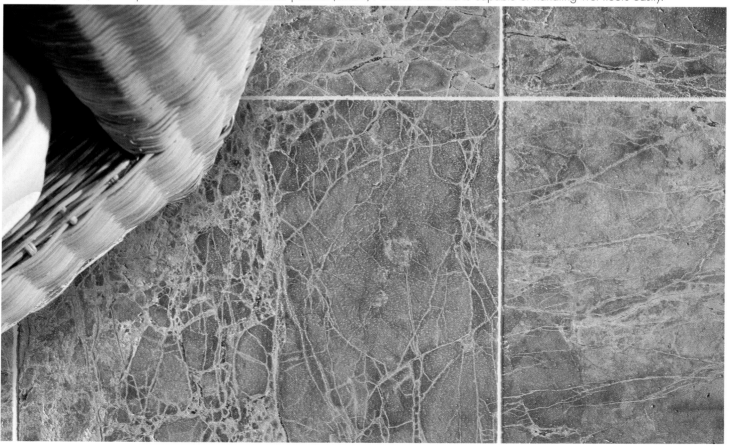

(above) Limestone mosaic draws eyes to the floor. (below) Natural slate shows varied colorations.

Gleaming ceramic tile sets off its main eye candy accessory.

Steps end in grand medallion.

Harlequin diamond pattern with fleur de lis accenting.

(above) Ceramic tile coupled with a tumbled stone mosaic accent.

Historic brickwork.   Concrete flooring treated with reactive acid stains.

Ceramic tile coupled with a tumbled stone mosaic accent.

12" x 12" tiles set diagonally.

(below) The sunny yellow tile tones with white cabinet accenting make an unbeatable combination.

Tea-stain finish glazed porcelain.

Beautiful high polish 12" x 12" squares.

Elaborate tile medallion.

Tusk-toned glazed ceramic tile.

Gleaming marble and accent detailing draw the eye.

Twelve inch ceramic tiles in varying tones.

Light beiges complement the wood-warm casegood.

Natural stone appeal with all the benefits of porcelain ceramic.

Natural cleft herringbone slate.

Thick, luxurious stone is as inviting as the water.

Rug pattern with varying earth-tone neutrals.

Entirely sophisticated; stunningly beautiful.

(above) Basaltina honed limestone on floor and treads. (below) Cleft slate slabs display beautiful, natural variations.

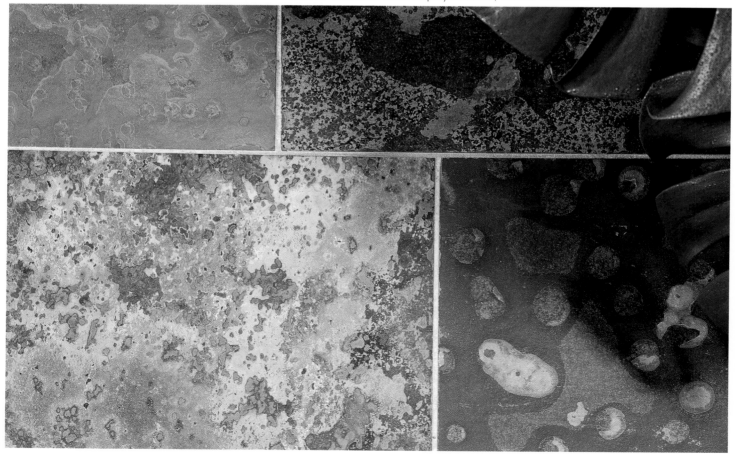

(above) Honed slate with moderate tone variations. (below) Mosaic limestone medallion displaying soft curves and gentle lines.

(above) Silver green honed slate will adapt to any situation, any surface.

Water tones abound in beautiful patterns and varied tones.

Glazed porcelain floor tile.

Soothing water tones of spruce and midori in 1" x 1" squares.

Clear glass has been sandblasted to an opaque finish.

(below) Glasstile, with up to 85% from recycled products.

Index

YOUR GUIDE TO EACH OF THE IMAGES YOU SEE ON the pages of this book. Enjoy!

All images listed read from right to left, top to bottom on the page.

> 1: In-Haus Flooring, inhaus-style.com; Chrisicos Interior Design, chrisicos.com; Houles et Cie, houles.com; Armstrong World Industries, armstrong.com

> 2 & 3: Armstrong World Industries, armstrong.com; Sarah Barnard Designs, sarahbarnard.com; Chrisicos Interior Design, chrisicos.com; Armstrong World Industries, armstrong.com

> 5: Seabrook, seabrookwallpaper.com

> 6 & 7: Sarah Barnard Designs, sarahbarnard.com; Shutterstock.com; Sarah Barnard Designs, sarahbarnard.com; Shutterstock.com

> 8 & 9: Sarah Barnard Designs, sarahbarnard.com

> 10: Hunter Douglas Window Fashions, hunterdouglas.com; Comfortex Window Fashions, comfortex.com; Smith+Noble, smithandnoble.com; (next 2) Aveno Window Fashions, aveno.com; Hunter Douglas Window Fashions, hunterdouglas.com; (next 2) Comfortex Window Fashions, comfortex.com; Springs Window Fashions/Graber, springs.com;

> 11: Shutterstock.com; Hunter Douglas Window Fashions, hunterdouglas.com; Smith+Noble, smithandnoble.com; Hunter Douglas Window Fashions, hunterdouglas.com; Springs Window Fashions/Graber, springs.com; (next 2) Comfortex Window Fashions, comfortex.com; Hunter Douglas Window Fashions, hunterdouglas.com; Comfortex Window Fashions, comfortex.com

> 12: ADO USA, ado-usa.com; Photo courtesy of Interiors by Decorating Den, decoratingden.com, 800-dec-dens; Crab Apple Farm Interiors, crabapplefarm.com; Photo courtesy of Interiors by Decorating Den, decoratingden.com, 800-dec-dens; Boral Timber, boraltimber.com; Photo courtesy of Interiors by Decorating Den, decoratingden.com, 800-dec-dens; (next 2) Smith+Noble, smithandnoble.com; Seabrook, seabrookwallpaper.com

> 13: Digital Vision; Seabrook, seabrookwallpaper.com; (next 2) Smith+Noble, smithandnoble.com; Seabrook, seabrookwallpaper.com; Photo courtesy of Interiors by Decorating Den, decoratingden.com, 800-dec-dens; (next 2) Smith+Noble, smithandnoble.com; Photo courtesy of Interiors by Decorating Den, decoratingden.com, 800-dec-dens

> 14: Linda Yackle, My Window Designs; Shutterstock.com; Photo courtesy of Interiors by Decorating Den, decoratingden.com, 800-dec-dens; Crab Apple Farm Interiors, crabapplefarm.com; Photo courtesy of Interiors by Decorating Den, decoratingden.com, 800-dec-dens; Casa Fiora, casafiora.com, photo courtesy of Casa Fiora; ADO USA, ado-usa.com; Chrisicos Interior Design, chrisicos.com; Smith+Noble, smithandnoble.com

Split draw panel system on a 144" span.
Photo courtesy of The Shade Store

danmer.com; Comfortex Window Fashions, comfortex.com; Hunter Douglas Window Fashions, hunterdouglas.com

> 49: (first 2) Danmer Custom Shutters, danmer.com; istockphoto.com
> 50–53: all Shutterstock.com
> 54: Seabrook Wallcoverings, seabrook.com; The Shade Store, the shadestore.com
> 55: Photo courtesy of Interiors by Decorating Den, decoratingden.com, 800-dec-dens; Shutterstock.com
> 56: (first 2) Photo courtesy of Interiors by Decorating Den, decoratingden.com, 800-dec-dens; Armstrong World Industries, armstrong.com
> 57: (all) Photo courtesy of Interiors by Decorating Den, decoratingden.com, 800-dec-dens
> 58: BTX, btxinc.com; The Shade Store, theshadestore.com; Smith+Noble, smithandnoble.com
> 59: Houles et Cie, houles.com; Photo courtesy of Interiors by Decorating Den, decoratingden.com, 800-dec-dens; Seabrook Wallcoverings, seabrook.com
> 60: Shutterstock.com; (last 2) Photo courtesy of Interiors by Decorating Den, decoratingden.com, 800-dec-dens
> 61: (first 2) Photo courtesy of Interiors by Decorating Den, decoratingden.com, 800-dec-dens; Shutterstock.com
> 62: Photo courtesy of Interiors by Decorating Den, decoratingden.com, 800-dec-dens; Shaw Industries, shawfloors.com; Seabrook Wallcoverings, seabrook.com
> 63: Shutterstock.com; Armstrong World Industries, armstrong.com; Shutterstock.com
> 64: (both) Calico Corners, calico-corners.com
> 65: (both) Shutterstock.com
> 66: Shutterstock.com; (next 2) Calico Corners, calicocorners.com
> 67: Springs Window Fashions/Graber, springs.com; Calico Corners, calico-corners.com; Shutterstock.com
> 68: Sarah Barnard Design, sarah-barnard.com; Shutterstock.com
> 69: Chrisicos Interior Design, chrisi-cos.com; istockphoto.com
> 70: Shutterstock.com; Integraf, photo courtesy of National Wood Flooring Association, woodfloor.org; Shutterstock.com
> 71: Calico Corner, calicocorner.com; Springs Window Fashions/Graber, springs.com; Shutterstock.com
> 72: Shutterstock.com; Springs Window Fashions/Graber, springs.com; Calico Corner, calicocorner.com

> 73: Calico Corner, calicocorner.com; Shutterstock.com; Chrisicos Interior Design, chrisicos.com
> 74: Shutterstock.com; Dahli Brant, Capital Designs West
> 75: (both) Shutterstock.com
> 76: BTX Inc, btxinc.net; Wendy Richens, richensdesigns.com; Shutterstock.com
> 77: (all) Shutterstock.com
> 78: Shutterstock.com; Hunter Douglas Window Fashions, hunterdouglas.com
> 79: Shutterstock.com; Calico Corners, calicocorners.com
> 80: Armstrong World Industries, armstrong.com; (next 2) Shutterstock.com
> 81: Shutterstock.com; istockphoto.com; Smith+Noble, smithandnoble.com
> 82: BTX Inc, btxinc.net
> 83: Photo courtesy of Interiors by Decorating Den, decoratingden.com, 800-dec-dens; (last 2) Shaw Industries, shawfloors.com;
> 84 & 85: Shutterstock.com
> 86: Hunter Douglas Window Fashions, hunterdouglas.com
> 87: Hunter Douglas Window Fashions, hunterdouglas.com; Comfortex Window Fashions, comfortex.com; Hunter Douglas Window Fashions, hunterdouglas.com
> 88: Shutterstock.com; Legacy Blinds, retroblinds.com; Comfortex Window Fashions, comfortex.com; Alta, altawindowsolutions.com
> 89: Photo courtesy of Interiors by Decorating Den, decoratingden.com, 800-dec-dens; Shutterstock.com; The Shade Store, theshadestore.com; shutterstock.com
> 90: Shutterstock.com; Springs Window Fashions, springs.com; Legacy Blinds, retroblinds.com
> 91: Shutterstock.com; Smith+Noble, smithandnoble.com; Shutterstock.com
> 92: The Shade Store, theshadestore.com
> 93: Springs Window Fashions/Nanik, springs.com
> 94: The Shade Store, theshadestore.com
> 95: BTX Inc, btxinc.net
> 96: Springs Window Fashions/Nanik, springs.com; Legacy Window Fashions, retroblinds.com; The Shade Store, theshadestore.com; Legacy Window Fashions, retroblinds.com
> 97: (first 2) Springs Window Fashions, springs.com; (last 2) Springs Window Fashions/Nanik, springs.com
> 98: The Shade Store, theshadestore.com
> 99: Photo courtesy of Interiors by Decorating Den, decoratingden.com,

800-dec-dens; Springs Window Fashions/Nanik, springs.com
> 100: Photo courtesy of Interiors by Decorating Den, decoratingden.com, 800-dec-dens; Comfortex Window Fashions, comfortex.com; Armstrong World Industries, armstrong.com;
> 101: Alta, altawindowsolutions.com; The Shade Store, theshadestore.com; Alta, altawindowsolutions.com
> 102: Danmer Custom Shutters/ Mermet; danmer.com
> 103: (all) The Shade Store, theshade-store.com
> 104: Fua Window Coverings, fuawin-dowcoverings.com
> 105: The Shade Store, theshadestore.com
> 106: Hunter Douglas Window Fashions, hunterdouglas.com; Springs Window Fashions/Graber, springs.com
> 107: Hunter Douglas Window Fashions, hunterdouglas.com; Alta, altawindowso-lutions.com; (last 2) Springs Window Fashions/Graber, springs.com
> 108: (first 2) Hunter Douglas Window Fashions, hunterdouglas.com; Alta, altawindowsolutions.com
> 109: Hunter Douglas Window Fashions, hunterdouglas.com
> 110: Shutterstock.com; Photo courtesy of Interiors by Decorating Den, deco-ratingden.com, 800-dec-dens; Castec, Inc., castec.com
> 111: (first 2) Photo courtesy of Interiors by Decorating Den, decoratingden.com, 800-dec-dens; CC's Designs, ccsdes@comcast.net, photo by Richard Leo Johnson
> 112: Photo courtesy of Interiors by Decorating Den, decoratingden.com, 800-dec-dens
> 113: Photo courtesy of Interiors by Decorating Den, decoratingden.com, 800-dec-dens; (last 2) Shutterstock.com
> 114: Shutterstock.com
> 115: Calico Corners, calicocorners.com; Smith+Noble, smithandnoble.com
> 116: The Shade Store, theshadestore.com; Calico Corners, cal-icocorners.com
> 117: Shutterstock.com
> 118: Danmer Custom Shutters, dan-mer.com
> 119: The Shade Store, theshadestore.com
> 120: Shutterstock.com
> 121: M.A.P. Interiors, mapinteriors.com; The Shade Store, theshadestore.com; Hunter Douglas Window Fashions, hunterdouglas.com
> 122: Shutterstock.com
> 123: Sarah Barnard Designs, sarah-barnard.com; Shutterstock.com

Index, cont.

Index, cont.

Classic Décor, theclassicdecor.com; Chrisicos Interior Design, chrisicos.com; (next 3) Photo courtesy of Interiors by Decorating Den, decoratingden.com, 800-dec-dens; Digital Vision; Seabrook Wallcoverings, seabrook.com

> 282: (first 6) SA Maxwell, samaxwell.com; (last 3) Smith+Noble, smithandnoble.com
> 283: (first 6) Smith+Noble, smithandnoble.com; Armstrong World Industries, armstrong.com; Hunter Douglas Window Fashions, hunterdouglas.com; CC's Designs, ccsdes@comcast.net, photo by Richard Leo Johnson
> 284: Chrisicos Interior Design, chrisicos.com; Photo courtesy of Interiors by Decorating Den, decoratingden.com, 800-dec-dens
> 285: Shutterstock.com
> 286&287: Shutterstock.com
> 288: Photo courtesy of Interiors by Decorating Den, decoratingden.com, 800-dec-dens; Dahli Brant, Capitol Designs West, capitaldesignswest.com; Shutterstock.com
> 289: Florida Tile, fltile.com; Davis & Davis, davisrugs.com; Shutterstock.com
> 290: Michael Goldman, Classic Décor, theclassicdecor.com; Stroheim & Romann, stroheim.com; (last 2) Photo courtesy of Interiors by Decorating Den, decoratingden.com, 800-dec-dens;
> 291: Photo courtesy of Interiors by Decorating Den, decoratingden.com, 800-dec-dens; Seabrook Wallcoverings, ww.seabrook.com; Chrisicos Interior Design, chrisicos.com; Shutterstock.com
> 292: Chrisicos Interior Design, chrisicos.com
> 293: Shutterstock.com
> 294: Photo courtesy of Interiors by Decorating Den, decoratingden.com, 800-dec-dens; Digital Vision
> 295: (both) Photo courtesy of Interiors by Decorating Den, decoratingden.com, 800-dec-dens
> 296: (All) Shutterstock.com
> 297: (Both) Shutterstock.com
> 298: Photo courtesy of Interiors by Decorating Den, decoratingden.com, 800-dec-dens; Bradbury & Bradbury Wallcoverings, bradbury.com; Photo courtesy of Interiors by Decorating Den, decoratingden.com, 800-dec-dens
> 299: Seabrook Wallcoverings, seabrook.com; Bradbury & Bradbury Wallcoverings, bradbury.com; Jamie Gibbs & Associates, jamiegibbsassociates.com
> 300: (First 3) Shutterstock.com; Photo courtesy of Interiors by Decorating

> 301: (both) Shutterstock.com
> 302: Expanko Inc., expanko.com; Aged Woods, agedwoods.com; Shutterstock.com
> 303: Mohawk Industries, mohawk.com; Aged Woods, Shutterstock.com; Armstrong World Industries/Robbins, armstrong.com
> 304: Jamie Gibbs & Associates, jamiegibbsassociates.com; Photo courtesy of Interiors by Decorating Den, decoratingden.com, 800-dec-dens; Photo courtesy of the Pensacola Symphony Showhouse 2007, pcolasymphonyshowhouse.com; Shutterstock.com
> 305: Beth Hodges Soft Furnishings, bhodgesdec@aol.com, photo by Rob Garbarini; Photo courtesy of Interiors by Decorating Den, decoratingden.com, 800-dec-dens
> 306: Boral Timber, boraltimber.com; ADO USA, ado-usa.com; Alloc Inc., alloc.com
> 307: Armstrong World Industries, armstrong.com; Hunter Douglas Window Fashions, hunterdouglas.com; Lori Carroll & Associates, loricarroll.com
> 308&309: Shutterstock.com
> 310: Boral Timber, boraltimber.com; Mohawk Industries, mohawk.com; Boral Timber, boraltimber.com; Mohawk Industries, mohawk.com; Boral Timber, boraltimber.com; Armstrong World Industries/Hartco, armstrong.com; Goodwin Heart Pine, heartpine.com; Osh-Kosh Floor Designs, oshkoshfloors.com; Boral Timber, boraltimber.com;
> 311: Boral Timber, boraltimber.com; Eterna Hardwood Flooring, parquetsdubeau.com; Boral Timber, boraltimber.com; Trestlewood, trestlewood.com; Anderson Hardwood, andersonfloors.com; Aged Woods, agedwoods.com; (next 2) Boral Timber, boraltimber.com; Mohawk Industries, mohawk.com
> 312: Beaulieu of America, beaulieu-usa.com; Odegard, odegardcarpet.com; Shaw Industries, shawfloors.com; Mohawk Industries, mohawk.com; Jaipur Rugs, jaipurrugs.com; Capel, Inc., capelrugs.com; Liora Manne, lioramanne.com; Central Oriental, centraloriental.com; Tinnin Oriental, tinnin.com
> 313: Shaw Industries, shawfloors.com; Oriental Weavers, owarug.com; Beaulieu of America, beaulieu-usa.com; Bowron Sheepskin Co., bowron.com; Odegard, odegardcarpet.com; (next 3) Armstrong

World Industries, armstrong.com; Alloc, Inc., alloc.com

> 314: Armstrong World Industries, armstrong.com; (next 3) Alloc, Inc., alloc.com; Armstrong World Industries, armstrong.com; Quick-Step Flooring, quick-step.com; In-Haus Flooring, inhaus-style.com; Alloc, Inc., alloc.com; Globus Cork, corkfloor.com
> 315: Expanko Inc., expanko.com Forbo Linoleum, forbolinoleumna.com; Armstrong World Industries, armstrong.com; (next 2) AllState Rubber, allstaterubber.com; Congoleum Corp., congoleum.com; Armstrong World Industries, armstrong.com; (last 2) Amtico International, amtico.com
> 316: Ann Sacks, annsacks.com; Osh-Kosh Floor Designs, oshkoshfloors.com; Epro Tile, eprotile.com; Dal-Tile Corp., daltile.com; (next 2) Bisazza North America, bisazzausa.com; Mohawk Industries, mohawk.com; Artistic Tile, artistictile.com, photo courtesy of Artistic Tile; Dahli Brant, Capitol Designs West, capitaldesignswest.com
> 317: Bronzework Studio/Lowitz & Co., lowitzandcompany.com; Carina Works, Inc., carinaworks.com; Kirkstone, kirkstone.com; Laufen Ceramic Tile Co., laufenusa.com; Dal-Tile Corp., daltile.com; Metropolitan Ceramics, metroceramics.com; Artistic Tile, artistictile.com, photo courtesy of Artistic Tile; Kirkstone, kirkstone.com; Teresa Cox, teresacox.com
> 318: Shutterstock.com
> 319: (all) Photos courtesy of National Wood Flooring Association, woodfloor.org
> 320: Goodwin Heart Pine, heartpine.com; Pioneer Millworks, pioneermillworks.com; Armstrong World Industries, armstrong.com
> 321: Capella Wood Floors, capella.com; Armstrong World Industries, armstrong.com; Pioneer Millworks, pioneermillworks.com
> 322: Armstrong World Industries/Robbins, armstrong.com; Armstrong World Industries/Bruce, armstrong.com
> 323: Mohawk Industries, mohawk.com; Ekowood International/TSH Products, ekowood.com
> 324: Mohawk Industries, mohawk.com; Shutterstock.com; Photo courtesy of National Wood Flooring Association, woodfloor.org
> 325: Shutterstock.com; Osh-Kosh Floor Designs, oshkoshfloors.com; Anderson Hardwood Floors, andersonfloors.com
> 326: (first 2) Ekowood International/